# Final Edit

## The Final Hours of Your Final Draft

## Books by Chris Yavelow

### Author

*Final Edit, The Final Hours of Your Final Draft*
*Tree of Life (under the pen-name: Chris Loveway)*
*The Macworld Music and Sound Bible (C.P.A. Award Winner)*
*Harmonization—The Pedagogy of Nadia Boulanger*

### Co-Author

*Multimedia Power Tools*
*Mastering the World of QuickTime*

### Contributing Author

*Macintosh Virtual Playhouse*
*Making Music With Your Computer*
*The Music Machine*

### Opera Libretti

*The Passion of Vincent van Gogh*
*The Rogue*

### Graphic Novels

*The Green Book (under the pen-name: Chris Johnson)*

### Manuals

*Miroslav Vitous Symphonic Orchestra Samples Users' Manual*
*Music Macros Users' Manual*
*A Player's Guide to the Kurzweil 250*
*MegaTrack 2.0 Users' Manual*

# Final Edit

## The Final Hours of Your Final Draft

**50 Time-Saving Editing Techniques
Every Writer Needs to Know**

**Chris Yavelow**

SCIENCE OF WRITING

ASHEVILLE, NORTH CAROLINA

**ISBN: 978-1-937449-00-1**

**Published by:**

**An Imprint of YAV Publications**

**Asheville, North Carolina**

YAV books may be purchased in bulk for educational, business, or fund-raising, or sales promotional use. Contact us by email at Books@YAV.com or phone: 828-619-0250 or 866-8333-YAV.

Visit our websites:
ScienceOfWriting.com    and    YAVpublications.com

3  5  7  9  10  8  6  4

*Assembled in the United States of America*
*Typefaces: Gill Sans and Minion Pro*
*Published  October 2011*

# Dedication

To the authors of the books I have edited in the past and the authors of the books I will edit in the future.

## A Principle that Spans Disciplines and Centuries

"Less is more." —*Robert Browning (poet)*
1812–1889

"Less is more." —*Ludwig Mies van de Rohe (architect)*
1886–1969

"Less is more." —*William Zinsser (author, editor, teacher)*
1922–

# Contents

# Preface

I wrote this book to solve a problem: The more books I publish, the more books I must edit, and the more that other authors and publishers contract me to edit their books. Often, the so-called final drafts I receive do not come near to what I would consider to be a final draft, and this adds many hours to my labor—hours that end up costing the authors money while taking time from other books and projects, both theirs and mine.

One of the original purposes of computers was to save time—to do, in minutes or seconds, tasks that would otherwise consume hours or days. Perhaps because I was there at the transition from the non-computer era to the computer-centric life, the transformation was more evident to me. It had a pronounced effect upon my life.

From the invention of the first word processor, I have felt it obvious that document-level operations, that is, procedures that affect a manuscript in its entirety—for example, searching for all double-spaces and replacing them with single spaces—unleash the sort of power for which computers were made, while saving hours of mundane editing. Apparently this was not obvious to others.

Simple operations such as the global double-space-replacement mentioned above and the dozens of similar tips and tricks described in this book, can reduce a grueling three to four-week editing marathon to one that lasts a single day.

Ever since becoming involved in books professionally, I have maintained lists of shortcuts and other self-editing helps for writers whose books I was publishing, editing, or simply critiquing in the many writers' groups I attend. Those resources became the basis of much of the book you now are reading.

Even armed with shortcuts and self-editing helps, writers must make difficult decisions for many changes required during the editing process. To facilitate this decision-making, I developed an expert system—a type of software related to artificial intelligence that emulates the decision-making process of human experts. Among other things, this program contains the knowledge base of good writing practices as defined by the authors whose books are listed in Appendix II "Books About Writing." The software relates those principles to a body of writing—a corpus—consisting of the bestselling works of the past fifty years, weighted towards the current list of bestsellers to reflect changing preferences of readers. You can read more about that program at the end of this book.

Equipped with the results from twelve years of data-mining bestsellers, I am able to provide some hard and fast rules pertaining to edit decisions that otherwise might force you to stop in your tracks while the clock is ticking.

For these reasons and more, I give you *Final Edit, The Final Hours of Your Final Draft*. Whether you are writing for a traditional publisher, or a print-on-demand publisher, or you plan to self-publish; whether hardbound, paperback, or eBook; the tool you hold in your hand right now will save you much time and money. If you apply the steps detailed herein, you will not only reduce the time required for your final edit, but also increase the accuracy of your editing, allowing you to quickly return to the more important task: writing.

*—Chris Yavelow*
*August 31, 2011*
*Asheville, North Carolina*

# Introduction

This book is organized so that the first time you read it, you can learn the steps required to edit your final draft as quickly as possible by applying those steps in the order they are presented while you read. Many of the steps require you to have performed the previous steps and may not function correctly otherwise. These will be clearly labeled.

Once you have become familiar with the editing techniques described herein, you may feel comfortable enough with the process to simply run through the list of searches near the end of the book. After you have edited several books in this manner, you might not need the list.

You may already have some expertise with some of the tools I present—as an editor and publisher I've discovered there are many personal definitions for the phrase "fluency with Microsoft Word." Some people who claim proficiency with Word have never read the manual (horrors!). For this reason, you may be able to skip some of the rudimentary explanation.

No matter what your level, I have designed *Final Edit—The Final Hours of Your Final Draft* so that you can read it and apply it to your manuscript in less than twelve hours. If this book seems too thick for that claim to be true, keep in mind that the beginning pages consist of background and basic information that you may choose to skip and, an even greater portion at the end of the book is devoted to reference chapters and appendices.

In between those "optional" sections, you will find the logically ordered step-by-steps that take you through search patterns to improve the form of your work: patterns for basic cleanup, finding and replacing problematic punctuation, repairing mismatched styles, and dealing with dialogue, for example.

The optional "Advanced Searches" section will help you deal with issues pertaining to the content of your manuscript: using search patterns for rapid rewrites, and to avoid redundancies, flab phrases, nominalization (verbs and adjectives with suffixes added to create nouns), and more.

If you want to go further, you can. The closing section will show you how to tune your searches to target "power position" elements (as described in Nancy Kress' excellent book *Beginnings, Middles, and Ends;* amzn.to/BeginningsMiddlesEnds) and focus on chunk endings to magnify the page-turner components that will drive your reader through your book.

You will discover that using search patterns to edit allows you to approach your work from a level of abstraction offering a degree of objectivity that is impossible to attain in any other way. When you read your own work consecutively, in the order the events of your story unfold, you are drawn into the plot and become too involved in your own story to edit it effectively.

The *Final Edit* approach speeds you through the editing process by having you make multiple passes through your work, focusing on one issue at a time. This is far more efficient than slowly plodding through your manuscript trying to notice every type of mistake imaginable, all at once. It is almost impossible to concurrently address errors that occur on multiple levels and in different domains, for example, form and content.

The 50 searches detailed in this book will scavenge your draft for thousands of errors and sometimes even fix the errors automatically. Rather than attempting to discern hundreds of categories of errors with every word you read, you will be focused on a single type of error until every instance of that error has been resolved. Because the searches herein take you from one error to the next error of that type, ignoring the material in between, you will drop into your draft only where there are problems that need to be fixed. This prevents you from being distracted by your own narrative, a state of affairs that can seriously impede self-editing.

When you have finished your final edit, you will be led through less than an hour of final steps (Chapter 11) to optimize your manuscript for book-design, eBook-conversion, or submission to an agent or publisher.

At the end of the book are Appendices containing a variety of references, including a categorized list of all the URLs mentioned in the book, a recommended reading list in the form of easy-to-use "amzn.to" links, for example: amzn.to/OnWritingWell (you should not add "www." before such links), and a handy, properly ordered "Index to Searches" that you can use as a checklist for subsequent searches, once you've mastered this process.

To learn the *Final Edit* editing process as quickly as possible, you will want to refer to the book repeatedly while editing. If you are reading this as an eBook using eBook-reader emulator software, you may want to quickly head to ScienceOfWriting.com to purchase a paper copy of the book. Your editing will be speedier and far easier to accomplish if you keep the book open while you edit on your screen. With this in mind, unless you are using a standalone eBook-reader, I recommend that you purchase the printed version of the book.

Whether you restrict yourself to basic editing or go through the *Final Edit* entire process, your book will be better for it. You will have a file that is ready to submit to an agent, publisher, POD, or book designer, and as a bonus, you will have a file that is also ready for immediate eBook conversion.

As a bonus, performing the steps in this book will present your most frequent mistakes to you, mercilessly, one after another. If you can learn from your mistakes, this will be a good thing. Having your errors displayed so rapidly and thoroughly will teach you not to make the same ones in your next book. The simple act of repeatedly correcting the same errors can help break deeply ingrained bad writing habits. The next time you reach the *Final Edit* stage, you may find that the process takes far less time.

## Before You Begin, Register This book

The information in this book has evolved over decades and there is every reason to expect that it will continue to evolve. Software changes. Some material may need to be revised or updated from time to time. To make sure that you are kept up-to-date, go to the ScienceOfWriting.com website and register this book. Registering your book will assure that receive you the following benefits:

1) You will be emailed an announcement when the next edition of this or other Science of Writing books are about to be published.

2) You will receive an announcement when software is released that will allow you to accomplish many of the tasks in this book automatically—software than can save you even more time.

3) You will have access to the User-Forums where you can participate in discussions about the final hours of your final draft.

4) You will be entered in our eBook-reader Give-Away. For every 1,000 copies of this book that are sold, whether paperbound or electronic, Science of Writing (an imprint of YAV Publications) will give away a free eBook-reader: a Kindle or a Nook—your choice. However, considering the changing landscape of eBook-readers, we reserve the right to substitute another eBook-reader in the unlikely event that another reader is better than either of those.

Have your book close by when you register, because you will be asked to enter a number from the book in order to verify that you truly own it.

We will not sell your email address nor will we give it away. We will use your email address only for the purposes mentioned above. If another YAV-related purpose arises, we will ask your permission before applying your email to that as-yet-unimagined bonus.

## Back Up Your File Before You Start to Edit

Many of the searches you will perform during your *Final Edit* are document-level searches. You press the "Replace All" button and every instance of something is changed. Because all books are unique, the results may not be what you intended. With this in mind, make a backup copy with a different file name before commencing your *Final Edit*.

# Chapter One

# Now What?

You've finished your final draft, so what should you do now?

As a new author, you may be aware that your book needs editing. If you are a seasoned author, you understand that it is imperative for your manuscript to be edited before publication.

You may have heard of self-editing, read a book about it, or even taken a class in self-editing at a writers' conference. You may imagine that you learned everything you need to know about editing in your high school English class. You may even believe that your manuscript is already perfect.

Be forewarned that unless you are planning to publish you book, unedited, through a vanity press or an online Print-On-Demand (POD) mill—such outfits customarily publish anything and everything sight unseen and without inspection—then your book will need to undergo some form of editing before it appears in print. Moreover, regardless of whether you plan to self-publish, contract a digital publisher (using POD or other types of digital printing), publish an eBook or have a whopping advance from an established, conventional publishing house, you will be the one who pays for the editing (see the section titled "Sample Editing Fees" in the upcoming chapter).

Don't get me wrong; editing your book is a good thing. In the long run, a well-edited book will receive much better reviews and achieve far greater sales. However, editing a substantial chunk of text in the traditional manner—line by line—can take two or more weeks. Self-editing is often hindered by the simple fact that authors tend to overlook their own mistakes.

## Current Prices of Freelance Editors

Without *Final Edit*, the editing fee for most books will be greater than $2,000 and often around $6,000 or even more. This is a one-time fee with most digital print publishers and POD publishers, and if you are self-publishing. But, with a "traditional" publisher, you will pay much more for the editing, and they will force you to continue to pay for it year after year, in the guise of reduced royalties.

For a conventional publisher, the pre-publication production processes such as editing and book design are regarded as being analogous to the costs of building an interstate highway. After the highway has been built, tollbooths or state taxes take your hard-earned money to pay for it or to pay for its annual maintenance. Once the builders have paid off their production costs and accumulated enough fund to cover annual highway maintenance for the next century, they should remove the tollbooths or reduce the highway taxes. Have you ever heard of that happening? The situation is the same with conventional publishers and books. If your book sells, it will have paid off the production costs very quickly. Moreover, because most marketing expenses occur in the first 6 weeks or months (in rare cases, up to a year), the publisher incurs few real "maintenance" costs. Caveat: keeping your book in catalogs may cost up to $100 per year. You might think that the logical thing would be to raise your royalty rate after all their expenses have been paid. Ask around. That never happens. It is precisely like a tollbooth that never gets removed. It's a cash cow for those collecting the money. And you're the one paying the bill.

*Final Edit* can save you all or most of your editing costs, and, in doing so, you might even be able to negotiate a higher royalty rate if your book is to be published by a traditional publisher.

For real world prices, current at the time of this writing, see Appendix III "The Cost of Editing." There you will find the average fees for various types of editing as reported by the Editorial

Freelancers Association (the EFA). To make these fees easier to relate to your own work, the figures have been converted to per-word fees. Examples of non-EFA editors are also provided, as our the rates of add-on editing services offered by large online print on demand mills.

A search of the web can verify that unless you do your final edit yourself, you will pay between $2,000 to $8,400 or more for the editing of your 100,000-word manuscript. Ask yourself whether you would rather spend the day that it will require for you to go through the steps in this book or spend thousands of dollars?

## Before the Final Hours

### The question you are probably asking yourself:

"Is my manuscript far enough along to be considered a 'final draft' for the purposes of this book?"

### The answer to your question:

*Final Edit—The Final Hours of your Final Draft* is designed to be used after you have run your spell-check and grammar check and *after* your developmental editing, after you have fixed any point of view problems, checked for consistency of viewpoint (omniscient, first-person, third-person, multiple, etc.), adjusted your chronology to the laws of the physical universe, logically ordered any cause–effect and action–reaction (including stimulus–response and expectation–fulfillment) elements, set the proper pacing, filled any holes in your plot, added your subplots and ticking clocks, removed all your authorial intrusions, inserted any missing transitions, deleted unnecessary back-story, trimmed excessive narration (particularly in second person), checked your flashbacks, corrected your diction and dialect, removed or clarified any jargon, resolved unintended *deus ex machina*, toned down all your "purple prose" (excessive description using a grandiose extravagance of adjectives), corrected any mixed metaphors, verified the appropriateness of clichés, expanded your sensory triggers, finalized your hooks, added your foreshadows and symbols, raised the stakes, and optimized all your scenes, summaries, sequels, and Motivation-Reaction Units (see the books by Nancy Kress and Dwight Swain in the Appendix for more information about these terms).

In short, the techniques detailed herein are designed to refine your work to its maximum level of perfection. In many cases, this will be *after* you believe that your draft requires no additional changes.

## A Revolutionary Approach to Editing

This book will show you how easy it is to leverage the advanced options of Microsoft Word (or similar word processors), such as Find and Replace with wildcards, to edit your book in a single day. As someone who once received the "Best Advanced How-To Book" award from the Computer Press Association, I am confident that my simple step-by-step tutorials will show you how to bring your editing not just to the next level, but several levels further.

And, if your book could talk, I guarantee that after you apply the steps in *Final Edit—The Final Hours of Your Final Draft*, your book would thank you for polishing both its form and content to allow it to step forth boldly into the world of ever more critical readers, with confidence that it will shine to its fullest potential.

# Chapter Two

# Essential Preparation

## Basic Setup (Word Preferences)

Before you take any of the *Final Edit* steps detailed in this book, you may want to execute a grammar and spell check. If you have been using Word's "Check spelling as you type" and "Check grammar as you type" options while writing your draft, you won't need to do this.

To do either of those operations effectively, I recommend setting your Preferences to the settings outlined in this chapter. Word's Preferences have many other settings, but those are omitted in the following lists because they either not relevant to the final edit or they concern personal preferences that have no impact on the matter at hand.

Note: In Word for Windows, the Preferences are called "Word Options."

Here's one example of why you should make sure your Preferences are set correctly. I was recently handed a manuscript and noticed that the first pages had sentences beginning with the word "On" in which the "O" was really a zero. I asked the author if he had run the manuscript through Word's grammar/spell checker. He assured me that he had. It turned out that he had left the "Ignore words with numbers" preference enabled. You may be surprised to discover that Word comes with that option enabled.

If you apply any of the Rapid Rewrite or Advanced Searches, and unless you are a seasoned grammarian, you may want to run a full grammar and spelling check at the end of the *Final Edit* process, too. You may be able to avoid this if you have enabled the "Check spelling as you type" and "Check grammar as you type" because certain errors will be displayed while you peruse your document, typically misspellings underlined with a dotted red underline and possible grammar errors underlined with a dotted green underline. All such errors should be examined. Even if you know that a spelling is unknown to Word, right-clicking on the questionable word or passage will allow you to ignore it for the rest of the document or add it to your custom dictionary so it will be ignored from that point forward in all documents.

Third-party grammar checkers and spell checkers are available, and in many cases, the more of this sort of technology you bring to bear upon your manuscript, the better it will be. I use Grammarian Pro from Linguisoft.com for quick inline Thesaurus and Dictionary operations, as well as getting a "second opinion" on grammatical issues in occasional ambiguous passages. Before deeming a manuscript to be completely final, I do consider all potential errors spotted by Word using the perusal method described in the previous paragraph.

You may be wondering why you need to worry about your Word Preferences at this stage. Isn't that something you should have done before you started writing in the first place? The answer is yes; however, there are other reasons to set your preferences according to the recommendations on the following pages. First and foremost is that some of the searches expect Word to respond in a specific way that can only occur if your Preferences have certain options enabled. As mentioned earlier, the Rapid Rewrite and Advanced Searches require you to type within your document, and whenever you do so, the possible of error is present. Other searches assume that double hyphens will be replaced by em dashes or that triple periods will be replace by genuine ellipsis characters.

Accessing your Preferences is easy on a Macintosh (press **command+comma** in practically any program, including Word), but this may not be the case for those using Windows. In Word for Windows 2007, click on the orb in the upper left corner of the frame. Next, click on the 'Word Options' button that appears. In

Word for Windows 2011, click the File tab and choose Options from the menu that appears.

When using Word on a Windows computer, you run a greater risk of inadvertently operating with Caps Lock enabled. You may want to use the free (donation-ware) utility MapKeyboard from Inchwest.com to disable your Caps Lock key.

The headings in the following lists refer to the names of the tabs in the Macintosh Preferences window and the list box items available in the Word Options window. A checkmark means that the item should be enabled, usually by clicking an "X" into a checkbox, and occasionally, by clicking upon a circular "radio button."

Note: In the following preference lists, some options are available only in Word 2011. These are indicated by (2011).

### Edit

√ Typing replaces selection *[*see note]*

√ Use smart cut and paste

      Settings (enable all defaults)

√ (2011) Keep track of formatting

√ Enable click and type

*\* Note:* Windows users should be careful not to confuse this option with the typing mode in which newly typed text overwrites existing (unselected) text—the opposite of "Insert Mode." The "Typing replaces selection" found in the Word Options (i.e., Preferences) refers to replacing highlighted (selected) text and then continuing in whatever mode you have currently activated, Insert Mode or otherwise. I have heard of problems with this due to unintended presses on the Insert key or by accidentally pressing **ALT+T**.

### Spelling and Grammar

√ Check spelling as you type

(uncheck) Ignore words in UPPERCASE

(uncheck) ignore words with numbers

√ Ignore Internet and file addresses

√ (2011) Flag repeated words

√ Check grammar as you type

√ Check grammar with spelling

Press the Settings button to configure you personal **Grammar Settings.** I recommend starting with the Standard options and enabling additional options, as you require. You will probably end up with a configuration that is somewhere between Standard and Formal. For example, you may want to enable the Numbers option; this will automatically spell out numbers that should be spelled out instead of written in numerals.

Depending upon whether you write fiction or nonfiction, some other options you might want enable, instead of selecting the full-blown "Formal" configuration, include:

Sentence Structure
Clichés
Successive prepositional phrases (more than three)
Wordiness
Words in split infinitives (more than one)

Below the Grammar Settings checkbox list, you will find at least three additional options to select:

1) Comma required before last list item: always
2) Punctuation required with quotes: don't check
3) Spaces required between sentences: 1

For additional explanation about specific options use Word Help or visit http://support.microsoft.com/search/?adv=1.

Note: All URLs mentioned in this book are collected in Appendix I "Link List."

### AutoCorrect — "AutoCorrect Tab"

√ Automatically correct spelling and formatting as you type
√ Show AutoCorrect smart button
√ Correct TWo INitital CApitals
√ Capitalize first letter of sentences *(uncheck while editing)*
√ Capitalize names of days

### AutoCorrect — "AutoFormat as you Type" Tab

**Apply as you type**
√ Headings
√ Automatic bulleted lists
√ Automatic numbered lists

**Automatically set as you type**
√ Tabs and backspace set left indent
√ Format beginning of list item exactly like the one before it

**Replace as you type**
√ "Straight quotation marks" with "smart quotation marks"
√ Ordinals (1$^{st}$) with superscript
√ Fractions (1/2) with fraction character (½)
√ Symbol characters (---) with symbols (—)
        *[see boxed note on next page]*
√ *Bold* and _italic_ with real formatting
NO = Internet and network path with hyperlinks

Other preferences you might find helpful:

### Save
- √ Always create backup copy
- √ Save preview picture with new documents
- √ Save auto-recover info every 5 minutes

### Compatibility

First select the "Defaults for Word 2007-2008" and then add the following:

- √ Suppress extra line spacing at top of page
- √ Suppress Space Before after a hard page or column break
- √ Swap left and right borders on facing pages

### Track Changes
Inserted text
Mark: Underline, Color: Teal
Deleted text
Mark: Strikethrough, Color: Red
Changed formatting
Mark: (none), Color: Blue
Changed lines
Mark: Outside border, Color: Auto
Comments
Color: By author
√ (2011) Track Moves
    (Use the defaults)

---

## Important Note About Symbol Character Replacement
**This pertains to the "AutoCorrect" option to "Replace as you type" "Symbol characters (--) with symbols (—):**

First, you should be aware that this also automatically replaces other symbols such as **three periods** with an **ellipsis** character. However, these automatic replacements do not occur in the Find & Replace box. No matter whether you are in wildcard mode or not, when you type two hyphens or three periods in the "Find what" field or the "Replace with" field, they will not be replaced by an em dash or an ellipsis. It is very important that you keep this in mind.

## Common Mistakes

As an editor, there are some mistakes I see repeatedly. Consider the following list as commandments to effective manuscript formatting. Most of the following errors will be fixed by using the Find and Replace patterns detailed in the rest of the book.

**Do not use double spaces between sentences**. This practice harkens back to the days of typewriters, before proportional fonts—the era when all characters were the same width. Adding an extra space between sentences was deemed to increase readability. Ever since 1984, the year that saw the maturation of personal computers to a level of user-friendliness that permitted wide-scale use, word processors have used proportional fonts: characters have different widths. The reader's eyes don't need helps such as double-spaces anymore; in fact, many people find it more difficult to read a passage with double-spaces between sentences. The global double-space replacement pattern was discussed in the Preface.

**Do not format with spaces.** This includes indenting paragraphs, outlines, or lists, as well as using spaces to center titles, headings, and subheadings. There is no reason to use more than a single space at a time, ever.

**Do not format with tabs.** As with spaces, this includes indenting paragraphs, outlines, or lists, as well as using tabs to center titles, headings, and subheadings. You may feel compelled to press the tab key to create an indent out of habit, but there are far better ways to accomplish the same thing. The best approach and one that we will discuss at length later in this book is to use *styles*. Another approach that was covered in the previous section titled "Basic Setup," is to use Word Preferences to designate that the tab key sets the left margin.

**Do not use multiple returns except in strictly defined cases.** Never use both indents combined with double returns to separate paragraphs. For non-fiction you are allowed to indent paragraphs or place extra space between paragraphs, *but not both*. For fiction, you don't have those choices—paragraphs are indented rather than double-spaced.

There is a occasional exception to that rule for fictional works: you may separate two paragraphs with a double return if there is a logical break, such as a shift of POV, location, or time, or any combination thereof. To greater emphasize such shifts, you may want to add a typographical ornament, sometimes called a dingbat, between paragraphs. It may be easiest to type two returns, and then add the centered ornament followed by another two returns. It is perfectly acceptable to have a hierarchy of such hiatuses, with a double-space being lower on the hierarchy than a space with a dingbat.

You may want to separate chapter headings and subheads with an extra return, too, and that's OK, too. Eventually, you or the book designer will use styles that assign absolute spacing both before and after such elements. The important thing is to be consistent. We will detail search patterns to optionally fix multiple returns in the chapter titled "Paragraphs and Sentences."

**Do not use manual line breaks except in strictly defined cases.** Many people use manual line breaks to repair problems that would not exist if they knew how to use styles. However, some situations do exist in which manual line breaks solve otherwise unsolvable formatting problems in Word. These cases pertain mainly to bulleted and numbered lists.

**Don't use any line spacing options in Paragraph Settings that are not exact.** For example, do not use "Multiple 1.15" or "At Least 1.25" because (unbeknownst to most Word enthusiasts) these settings override style settings in most versions of Word. If a document has sections with, for example a line-spacing setting of "Multiple 1.15" and you apply a style to that paragraph that uses a line-spacing setting of "Exactly 15 pts," the sections with the "Multiple of…" line-spacing will not be altered. "Multiple" takes precedence over "Exactly." The settings "Single," "1.5," "Double," and "Exactly" are all considered by Word to be of lesser importance than "Multiple" and "At Least," and this negates the power of styles, which is something you do not want to happen.

**Don't use drop caps, just tell the book designer you'd like them.** Your book designer (or you, if you are your book designer) will likely be formatting and reformatting the first paragraphs of all your chapters, as well as any other sections you might have gone overboard on while you are supposed to have been writing. This formatting and reformatting will probably include a font change and maybe even a change of size and/or leading (line-spacing). Such changes will require most drop caps that you created to be removed and redone. The time wasted during the removal process will add expense.

## Recommendations (Styles, Styles, Styles)

Styles are a feature of Word and most other word processing programs such as Pages and Scrivener (in which they are called Presets). Styles allow you to define a style—a look or appearance— of document elements that includes everything from font characteristics like weight and font size, to indents, line spacing, margins, tabs, alignment, page breaks, and much more. Styles can apply to individual characters and words or to entire paragraphs, or both.

Examples of the most basic of these are a *Chapter Heading* style and a *Body Text* style. You might want separate styles for the *Chapter Number, Block Quotes,* and *Footnotes.*

Once you have assigned a style to, for example, a chapter heading, you can specify that after you've typed the chapter heading and pressed return, the next style will automatically be *Body Text* and that the *Body Text* style will always follow *Body Text* (again, unless overridden by you when you start a new chapter). Styles are not difficult once you've set them up to logically follow one another.

The true power of styles lies in that when you have finished your manuscript and are in the book design phase (or your book designer begins his or her task), simply changing the style once changes all occurrences of that style. If you decide that you would rather use 32-point Helvetica Bold for your chapter headings, simply change the font of one heading and all the other headings will change accordingly. Actually, this is what happens if the "Automatically Update" checkbox is enabled in the style definition dialog box, otherwise, you can mouse-down upon the name of the style assigned to the currently selected text in the "Pick style to apply" for a popup menu with the option to "Update to Match Selection." Selecting this option will have the same effect as having set your styles to automatically update.

You can have as many styles as you like in most word processors, but it is a good idea to keep it simple. It's an even better idea to define and assign styles that will be meaningful in any subsequent conversion of your book to an eBook.

### No Styles in your document yet?

If you haven't set up styles yet in your document, you should wait until you have finished your final edit. Immediately following the final search is a chapter titled "Final Steps." That chapter will walk you through assigning styles and even use some of the expertise you will have acquired by then to leverage the Find & Replace box to automatically assign several of your styles.

### Styles and Special Formatting Requirements

If your intent is to submit your edited manuscript to an agent, publisher, or a competition, you may be asking yourself why you need to use styles or you may be worried that styles may present a problem because the person to whom you are going to send your final draft has requested that your manuscript be in double-spaced, 12-point Courier or Times New Roman. Don't worry, in such cases simply "Select All" and change the font to the one requested, the size requested, and the line spacing requested (and anything else that may have been requested, such as margin settings). If your styles are set to "Automatically Update," then your manuscript will print just fine. If your styles are not set to "Automatically Update," you will have to mouse-down on each one and select "Update to Match Selection" from the popup menu, a process that may take all of five minutes. You should save it as a "copy," in either scenario. The good news is that in either case you will retain a copy that will save you considerable expense from the book designer and also the eBook compiler, or save considerable time, if you plan to do either or both of these tasks. Another benefit is that even though the overall look of your document—font family, font size, line spacing, and more—is now the same throughout, all your centering and indents remain intact.

### Learning to Use Styles

It is not the purpose of this book to teach you how to create styles, however, it is in our interests for you to save time and money. For that reason, we've included this brief introduction to styles at this stage, but follow up with a more detailed explanation in Chapter 11, "Final Steps."

If you want to learn more about using styles in Word, the resources in the Link List Appendix provide an excellent place to start. There, you will find URLs linked to step-by-steps for learning how to create styles in Word 2010/2011 and 2007/2008, as well as video tutorials that will teach you how to use styles in about a half hour.

# Chapter Three

# Introducing Search

## Find and Replace

You've probably used Word's Find function to navigate through your manuscript as its number of pages increased. You may have used Find and Replace before, perhaps to change a character's name. And you may have explored some of the more advanced formatting options to, for example, convert all mentions of a book title to italic or to capitalize a phrase you thought was lowercase.

By the time you finish this book, you may look at Word's Find and Replace with new respect. You may even consider it to be the most important part of the program, even more valuable than styles.

I liken the experience to one I once had when I rented a BMW to drive from Basel, Switzerland, to Cherbourg, France. There was a little button on the gearshift. I assumed it was the same as the little buttons I was used to on American cars, that is, to prevent one from accidentally shifting into reverse—in other words, nothing of consequence. Imagine my surprise when I pressed that button and found it enabled the car to go about twice as fast as I was going. After pressing that button, I made the trip in record time, traveling between 200 kph to 240 kph (120 mph to 150 mph); this was before European highways had speed limits. Using the techniques described in this book will have the same effect upon your final edit.

## Two Types of Find/Replace: Global vs. Selective

To accomplish our light-speed final edit, we will use two types of Find and Replace (bold text refers to the button names in the upcoming screenshots): 1) **Replace All:** Global replacements act upon the document as a whole and do not require your confirmation before changing individual "hits"; and 2) **Find Next** used in conjunction with **Replace:** These selective replacements require you to decide whether or not to replace each find.

## Global Replacements: Single Step vs. Multiple Step

Global replacements may consist of a single step, initiated by a single button-press, or they may include multiple steps.

### Example: Global Double-space Replacement (later called #1a)

The first example we will consider is the simplest of all searches: a single step global replacement. This search replaces of all double spaces by single spaces. In the next chapter, you will learn a more efficient way to perform this search.

1) Type two spaces in the "Find what" field

2) Type one space in the "Replace with" field

3) Press the "Replace All" button. If necessary, repeat until the results box says "Word has completed its search of the document and made 0 replacements."

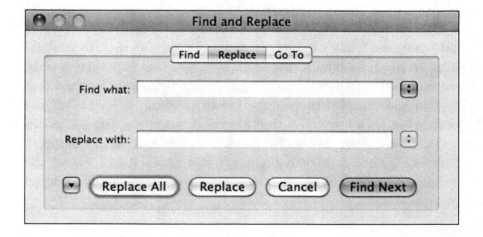

The problem with the previous illustration is that there is no way to see the two space characters in the "Find what" field, and there is no way to see the single space character in the "Replace with" field. Because of this, most of the searches that use the space character will indicate its presence with the word **space** (in the font assigned to Find and Replace field characters). When the search involves wildcards, **space** will be indicated by **caret+32** (i.e. **^32**) which is another way to represent a **space** character. More about this at the end of this chapter.

### Example: Global 3-Step Return Replacement (later called #3)

An example of a 3-step replacement is repairing a manuscript in which the author has placed a return at the end of each line and a double return after each paragraph. We use the global 3-step Return Replacement:

---

1) Replace all double returns with a placeholder such as %% (Two percent signs never occur consecutively so we use them as place holders. These will later become the real returns in the document).

2) Replace all returns with a single space. Later we will convert any double spaces created in this step to single spaces. We now have a document with no returns anywhere; it is simply one big block of text.

3) Replace all placeholders (%%) with return.

---

See the next page for screenshots showing the three steps. The first box shows two returns (^p^p) being replace by to percent signs (%%) as a placeholder. The next box shows any remaining returns (^p) being replaced by nothing (The "Replace with:" field is empty). The third box shows all the original double returns, now represented by two percent signs being restored to single returns by replacing the placeholders (%%) with single returns (^p).

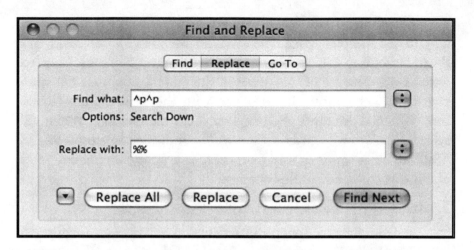

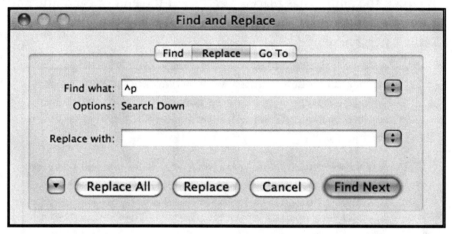

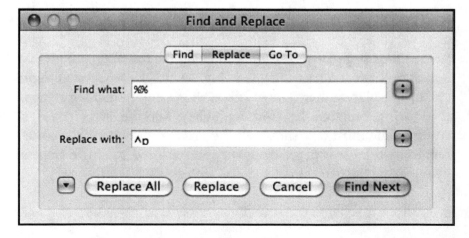

## Selective Replacements: Single Option vs. Multiple Option

Selective Replacements require that you make a decision about the replacement. Usually, your decision will involve one optional replacement. Using Word, you can also toggle between two replacements (or none) for each found text. Adding third-party macro-making software such as Keyboard Maestro for the Mac or AutoHotKey for Windows can enable you to choose from many different replacements for your found text. A clipboard manager to provide multiple clipboards can be substituted for or added to the aforementioned macro-making software.

## Example: Single-Option Replacement

In this case you will stay inside the Find & Replace box and Replace, having positioned it so that you can see your manuscript page, including the current found text, above or to the side. This allows you to base your decisions upon context. You alternate pressing the Find Next button, which finds the next occurrence of your "Find what" text, or the Replace button, which replaces the last found text with the contents of the "Replace with" field.

Here is an example of how to selectively replace some instances of "their" with "his or her":

1) Load your "Find what" field with the word "their"

2) Load your "Replace with" field with the phrase "his or her"

3) Press the Find Next button or the Replace button, as the found text requires.

## Example: Double-Option Replacement

Because recent versions of Word no longer use a modal dialog box for their Find & Replace box, you are able to keep the dialog box open and switch the active window back and forth from your manuscript window to your Find & Replace box. This allows you to keep alternate replacement text on your clipboard, thus giving you three options: 1) to replace the found text with the contents of the "Replace with" field; 2) to click on your manuscript window and press **Command+V** (on a Mac, abbreviated as **Cmd+V**) or **Control+V** (on a PC, abbreviated as **Ctrl+V**) to replace the found text with the contents of the clipboard; or 3) to simply press the "Next" button without replacing anything.

Here is an example of how to replace "they" with "Frankie and Johnnie" or "the two lovers":

> 1) Load your "Find what" field with "they"
>
> 2) Load your "Replace with" field with "Frankie and Johnnie"
>
> 3) Copy (or cut) "the two lovers" to your clipboard
>
> 4) Press the Find Next button or the Replace button to choose between the default replacement (Frankie and Johnnie) and retaining the word "they."
>
> 5) Whenever you want to replace the found text with the contents of the clipboard, click on the manuscript window to make it active. Then press Command-V (on a Mac) or Control-V (on a PC) to replace the found text with the contents of the clipboard ("the two lovers"). You will need to click the Find & Replace box to make it active and then press the Next button. This alternate replacement should be the one you expect to use least, because of the additional clicks.

You can expand the number of alternate choices to present many possibilities with a third party software clipboard manager.

This concludes our introduction to Find and Replace. Some of the replacements will be as easy as the examples in this chapter; most of them will not. It is important that you understand the basic search operations: Global and Selective, and that you understand both are used in several variations.

## Wildcards and More

The most important part of the Find & Replace box is a hidden area containing advanced Find and Replace options. To reveal this area in Word: Mac 2008, click on the disclosure triangle at the lower left of the dialog box. In Word: Mac 2011, choose "Advanced Find and Replace…" in the "Find" submenu under the "Edit" menu. In Word for Windows (2007), click "More" when in the normal "Find" box. In Word for Windows 2010, on the "Home" tab, in the "Editing" group, click the arrow next to "Find," and then click "Advanced Find."

You should see a horizontal divider named "Search" (Mac) or "Search Options" (Windows) and another below that named "Find" (both Mac and Windows).

Under "Search," is a popup menu for specifying scope. It includes the options "Current Document Down," "Current Document Up," "Current Document All," and "All Open Documents." (The last item is missing from Word Mac 2011, and is difficult to find in Word for Windows. We won't use it.) For now, choose "Current Document All" (Mac) or "All" (Windows).

Beneath the scope popup menu are checkboxes labeled "Match case," "Find whole words only," "Use wildcards," "Sounds like," and "Find all word forms." With the exception of "Use wildcards," these are self-explanatory. Windows users have a few more options (described on the next page).

## Using Wildcards

The option "Use wildcards" changes the items available by way of the "Special" menu. You don't need to memorize these (listed on the following pages), but you may want to make a mental note of where to find this information should you happen to need it later.

The most frequently used wildcards are gathered in the "Special" menu at the bottom of the "Find" area. These are listed in the left column of the upcoming table. The center column displays the symbol that Word will place in the "Find what" field when you select an item from that menu. You do not have to enable the "Use wildcards" checkbox to use these items from the "Special" menu; in fact, some won't work if "Use wildcards" is enabled.

Eventually, you may find that you have committed some of these options to memory and it will be faster to simply type the option in the "Find what" field, directly, rather than having Word enter it according to your selection from the "Special" menu.

One symbol you should commit to memory immediately is the caret symbol: ^. Many of the most powerful search options, whether using wildcards or not, are represented by a caret followed by a letter or number. You type this symbol by pressing **Shift+6**.

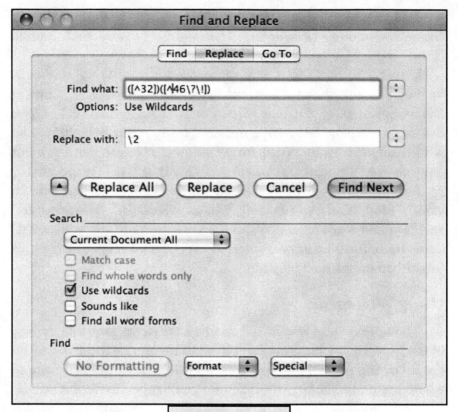

The buttons in the lower "Find" area may be in a different order if you are using Windows. The "Format" menu appears at the right. The options on the "Special" menu are discussed on the next page.

Font...

Paragraph...

Tabs...

Language...

Frame...

Style...

Highlight

In Windows, this side of the box may have four additional buttons:

1. Match prefix
2. Match suffix
3. Ignore punctuation
4. Ignore white-space

| Special Menu | | |
|---|---|---|
| Paragraph Mark (note 1) | ^p or ^13 | FW, RW, On, Off (note 2) |
| Tab Character | ^t or ^9 | FW, RW, On, Off |
| Comment Mark | ^a or ^5 | FW, Off |
| Any Character | ^? | FW, Off |
| Any Digit | ^# | FW, Off |
| Any Letter | ^$ | FW, Off |
| Caret Character | ^^ | FW, RW, On, Off |
| Column Break | ^n or ^14 | FW, RW, On, Off |
| Em Dash | ^+ | FW, RW, On, Off |
| En Dash | ^= | FW, RW, On, Off |
| Endnote Mark | ^e | FW, Off |
| Field | ^d | FW, Off |
| Footnote Mark | ^f or ^2 | FW, Off |
| Graphic | ^g | FW, On |
| Manual Line Break | ^l or ^11 | FW, RW, On, Off |
| Manual Page Break | ^m | FW, RW, On, Off |
| Nonbreaking Hyphen | ^~ | FW, RW, On, Off |
| Nonbreaking Space | ^s | FW, RW, On, Off |
| Optional Hyphen | ^- | FW, RW, On, Off |
| Section Break (see note 3) | ^12 | FW, RW, On, Off |
| Section Break (see note 4) | ^b | FW, Off |
| White Space | ^w | FW, Off |

Note 1:  ^p will not work when wildcards are enabled.
         ^13 will not work unless wildcards are enabled.
Note 2:  FW = can be used in the Find What field.
         RW = can be used in the Replace With field.
         On = can be used with wildcards enabled.
         Off = cannot be used with wildcards enabled.
Note 3:  ^12 will not work unless wildcards are enabled, and will
         insert a page break when replacing.
Note 4:  ^b will not work when wildcards are enabled.

| Other codes not on the Special menu: | | |
|---|---|---|
| ASCII Character | **^nnn** (nnn=character code) | FW, RW, On, Off |
| ANSI Character | **^0nnn** (0 = zero, nnn=character code) | FW, RW, On, Off |
| Unicode Character | **^unnn** ("u" followed by nnn for the char code) | FW, Off |
| Inline Picture or Graphic | **^1** | FW, Off |
| Em space (nicode) | **^u8195** | FW, Off |
| En space (nicode) | **^u8194** | FW, Off |
| Clipboard contents | **^c** | RW |
| Find What contents | **^&** | RW |

| Codes that require Field Codes to be visible: | | |
|---|---|---|
| ^Opening field brace | **^19** | FW, Off |
| ^Closing field brace | **^21** | FW, Off |

| Other "Find what" options with "Use wildcards" enabled | | |
|---|---|---|
| Single character | **?** | |
| Wildcard character This lets the character "escape from its wildcard function. | **\** | Precede the character with a backslash: **\?** Finds a question mark |
| One or more characters | ***** | |
| One of these characters | **[ ]** | |
| One character in a range | **[-]** | |
| Any character except these | **[!x-y]** | |
| At the beginning of a word | **<()** | |
| At the end of a word | **()>** | |
| One or more occurrences of the previous character or expression | **@** | |

| | | |
|---|---|---|
| NOT<br>(Place the exclamation mark as the first item within the brackets with the characters and/or ranges of characters to exclude.) | **[!]** | |
| *n* occurrences of the previous character or expression | **{n}** | |
| At least *n* occurrences of the previous character or expression | **{n,}** | |
| From *n* to *m* occurrences of the previous character or expression | **{n,m}** | |
| Use parentheses to create expressions of Wildcard characters | **( )** | **<(un)*(able)>** finds unbelievable and unthinkable |

With wildcards enabled, you can even use the Find & Replace box to manipulate the order of the words in the "Find what" field. If you type **(said)( )(Stuart)** in the "Find what" field and **\3\2\1** in the "Replace with" field, Word will replace occurrences of "said Stuart" with the reordered (and correct form) "Stuart said." The **\3\2\1** reverses the order of the 3 items in parentheses.

TIP: Attributions such as "said," "asked," "answered," "whispered," "shouted," and so forth must always come after the person who is doing the speaking. If you are in the habit of making this mistake, this is yet another *Final Edit* search pattern that you will find extremely useful. It will be covered in the chapter called "Search and Rapid Rewrite."

## The Fundamental Operation

Two fundamental operations are required by the two types of searches—Global and Selective—described in the previous chapter. The first is to press the Replace All button when executing one of the global searches. The second is to press either the Replace or Find Next buttons when doing one of the selective searches.

**Essential Keyboard Shortcuts (Commit to memory):**

| Commands to Open the Find & Replace box | | | |
|---|---|---|---|
| | **Mac OS** | **Windows** | **Word Command** |
| (1) Find | **Cmd+F** | **Ctrl+F** | EditFind |
| (2) Replace | **Opt+Cmd+F** **Shift+Com+H** | **Ctrl+Alt+F** | EditReplace |
| (3) Advanced Find and Replace (Word 2011) | (4) *[Cmd+F]* | (5) *[Ctrl+F]* | EditFindDialog |

| Shortcuts available when the Find & Replace box is Open | | | |
|---|---|---|---|
| Find Next | **Enter** | **Enter** | |
| Replace (and Find Next) | **Cmd+R** | **R** | |

| Shortcuts available when the Find & Replace box is Closed | | | |
|---|---|---|---|
| Find Next | **Cmd+G** **Opt+Cmd+Y** | **Ctrl+Alt+Y** | RepeatFind |
| Find Previous | **Shift+Cmd+G** | | EditFindPrevious |
| Replace (and Find Next) | | **Ctrl+H** | |
| Replace | (6) | (7) | |

| You will also need | | | |
|---|---|---|---|
| Paste | **Cmd+V** | **Ctrl+V** | EditPaste |
| Undo | **Cmd+Z** | **Ctrl+Z** | EditUndo |
| Copy | **Cmd+C** | **Ctrl+C** | EditCopy |
| Cut | **Cmd+X** | **Ctrl+X** | EditCut |

(1) to (7): See the notes on the next page.

(1) "Find" opens the Find & Replace box in Find mode (not very useful)

(2) "Replace" opens the Find & Replace box in Find & Replace mode (somewhat useful)

(3) There is no built-in keyboard shortcut for "Advanced Find and Replace," although this is the most useful option of all.

(4) and (5) Recommend using the "Customize Keyboard" menu option to remove **Cmd+F** (**Ctrl+F** in Windows) from the EditFind Word command, and assign it to Word's EditFindDialog command because you will be using this feature far more than the simple Find command.

(6) and (7) For Selective Replacements, you can effectively do a Replace while the Find & Replace box is closed by loading the Clipboard with your replacement text. Use **Cmd+G** (Apple) or **Ctrl+Alt+Y** (Windows) to find your search text. Then, use **Cmd+V** (Apple) or **Ctrl+V** (Windows) to replace the found text. Then, proceed to the next found chunk with **Cmd+G** (Apple) or **Ctrl+Alt+Y** (Windows). This adds a step, but it works, and it is the only way to simulate the Replace (and Find Next) on a Mac with the Find & Replace box closed. (Note: Sometimes you must perform the first search with the Find & Replace box open.)

Instead of using keyboard shortcuts, you may want to install some of the commands on a toolbar by using the View → Customize Toolbars and Menus… (Word 2007/2008) or View → Toolbars →Customize Toolbars and Menus… (Word 2010/2011). Installing commands on toolbars is simply a drag-and-drop operation. This will give you access to the "Find Next" command with a single mouse-click if you find that easier than using keyboard shortcuts.

If you do not know how to assign, de-assign, and reassign keyboard shortcuts in Word, you can find a step-by-step explanation and video tutorials in the Link List listed in the Appendices.

# How to Type Special Characters

Throughout *Final Edit* we will refer to special characters—em dashes, en dashes, ellipses, open quotation marks, close quotation marks, single quotes and double quotes, carets, curly brackets, and more. If you do not know how to type these characters, choose "Symbol..." from the "Insert" menu. You should see the following:

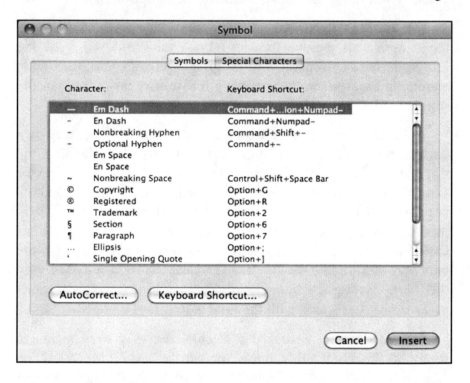

Word displays the default keyboard shortcut in the column on the right, but you can change these to something else by using the buttons "AutoCorrect..." and "Keyboard Shortcut..." at the lower left of the box.

As we get deeper into *Final Edit's* wildcard searches, you will often need to know a character or symbol's ASCII code. You can find that here, too. Simply click on the "Symbols" tab at the top of the box, select your font name, and click on the desired character in the font matrix. The ASCII code will be displayed right below the font matrix.

| How to Type Common Special Characters | | |
|---|---|---|
| Character | Mac OS | Windows (see note) |
| Em dash | Shift+Opt+Hyphen | Alt+0151 |
| En Dash | Opt+Hyphen | Alt+0150 |
| Ellipsis | Opt+Semicolon | Alt+0133 |
| Left Single Quote | Opt+] | Alt+0145 |
| Right Single Quote | Shift+Opt+] | Alt+0146 |
| Left Double Quote | Opt+[ | Alt+0147 |
| Right Double Quote | Shift+Opt+[ | Alt+0148 |

Note: The numbers following the **Alt** key may need to be typed on the numeric keypad when entering the special characters outside of the Find & Replace box. This restriction does not apply the same numbers when they appear in wildcard searches when they occur after a caret (^). For example, typing ^0148 in the "Find what" field with "Use wildcards" enabled will find em dashes.

**Re-read the "Important Note" on page 13 at this time.**

| Other Useful Character Codes | | |
|---|---|---|
| Character | Caret-based Code | Windows keyboard |
| space | ^32 | Alt+0032 |
| tab | ^12 | Alt+0012 |
| return | ^13 | Alt+0013 |
| period | ^46 | Alt+0046 |
| comma | ^44 | Alt+0044 |
| colon | ^58 | Alt+0058 |
| semicolon | ^59 | Alt+0059 |
| question mark (Windows only) | ^63 | Alt+0063 |
| exclamation mark (Windows only) | ^33 | Alt+0033 |
| foot (single straight quote) | ^39 | Alt+0039 |
| inch (double straight quote) | ^34 | Alt+0034 |

# Chapter Four

# Paragraphs and Sentences

## First Things First

Now we come to the main part of this book: the eight chapters devoted to the Find & Replace patterns that, taken together, make up the *Final Edit* process. The "Final Hours of Your Final Draft" begin right now. If you like, you can start your stopwatch.

We will remedy the common paragraphing mistakes by applying Replacement Searches in this chapter. Most of them are global. With any global search, you should stay in the Find & Replace box and press the Replace All button. After the replacement runs, you will be presented with the message "Word has completed its search of the document and has made *nnn* replacements" (*nnn* will be the number of replacements). If the number of replacements is greater than zero, repeat the search until the last two words are "0 replacements" (zero).

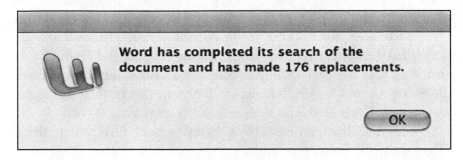

**Word has completed its search of the document and has made 176 replacements.**

OK

### *Two recommendations before you begin:*

Turn on the "Show Invisibles" option before executing any searches (You can toggle the invisibles on and off with a simple click on the toolbar's paragraph mini-icon). This will help you monitor your progress and increase your awareness of errors that might have been avoided during the writing process.

In each list of searches, including the searches in this chapter and those in forthcoming chapters, perform the searches *in the order they are presented.* Some of the replacements are constructed with the assumption that prerequisite repairs have been completed.

More importantly, if you are working against a deadline and may not be able to complete all the searches, the lists have been organized to present the most crucial searches and the ones that are the least time-consuming first. Because of this, the earlier searches favor global, single-button searches that can be accomplished with great speed, whereas the later searches are increasingly of the selective variety, which, by having to consider each found chunk individually, can be time-consuming.

As you become more comfortable with the different types of searches—global and selective versions of both wildcard and non-wildcard searches—you will realize which ones do not depend on earlier searches and can be executed out of sequence.

### Two Important Symbols You Need to Memorize

Because it is difficult to see whether a **space** character is part of a wildcard search string, whenever this is the case, instead of displaying a **space** in the example, the ASCII code **^32** will be used to make the expression easier to read. Don't forget the list of character codes on page 33, you will need to consult it occasionally.

As the searches become more advanced, sometimes a search string may extend over two lines. In such cases, the character ¬ indicates that the current line is continued on the next line. The ¬ character should be omitted when retyping the broken string of characters. The ¬ character does not imply a **return**.

Note that the contents of a "Find what" field entry or a "Replace with" field entry will be displayed in **this font.** Keyboard modifiers used in keyboard shortcuts also appear in the same font:

| Apple OS | Meaning | Windows OS |
|----------|---------|------------|
| Shift | Shift Key | Shift |
| Ctrl | Control Key | Ctrl |
| Opt | Option/Alt Key | Alt |
| Cmd | Command Key | |

---

### Important Note About Spelled-Out Punctuation.

In the search definitions that appear in the shaded boxes, sometimes you will see the words **space, return, period, comma,** and so forth in the font reserved for those words. Simply type the actual space, return, period, or comma rather than typing the word. Sometimes a plus sign is used with these, for example **space+space**. In this case, type two spaces without the plus sign.

---

## Let the Searches Begin!

### *Paragraph Repairs*

#### 1a) Global Double-space Replacement (Without the Special Menu)

**Comment**: This will ensure that your document contains no double-spaces, whether between sentences or for other unacceptable formatting reasons. Skip to the next search (Using the Special Menu) to perform this search more quickly.

> A. *Find what:* **space+space** (double space)
>
> *Replace with:* a single **space**.
>
> B. Repeat "A" until the search results come up as zero.

**Explanation**: See the next search for a better approach to this.

#### 1b) Global Double-space Replacement (Using the Special Menu)

**Comment**: This search accomplishes the same result as the previous search, but you can perform this search with a single click because the "white space" symbol represents an number of spaces.

> A. *Find what:* **space+^w** (caret+w means "white space")
>
> *Replace with:* **space** (a single space)
>
> B. Replace All (a single button click)

**Explanation**: The "Find what" field contains caret (^) followed by a lowercase "w." This **^w** represents any amount of white space, meaning any number of spaces in a row, even a single one. We replace all of them with a single space, leaving no instances of multiple spaces and requiring only one button click. The difference between this search and the previous one is that the first search required multiple button clicks (Repeat "A" until the search results come up as zero). Note that the **caret+w** pattern may be inserted by way of the Special menu by selecting "White Space."

## 2) Global or Selective Manual Line Break Replacement

**Comment**: This converts all manual line breaks (shift-returns) into normal returns. Read the notes below before performing this replacement.

> A. *Find what:* manual line breaks (**^l**), that is, a caret followed by a lowercase "L"
>
> B. *Replace with:* a single return **^p**, that is a caret follow by a lowercase "P"

This will replace manual line breaks (created by typing shift-return) with normal paragraph breaks. This replacement can be global or selective depending upon if and how you have used manual line breaks. There are some valid reasons for using these and they will not present problems to eBook conversion because they convert to the HTML tag </ br>, but they can be a nightmare for the book designer.

First scan your document to see whether you have used manual line breaks to override the effects of normal returns for a good reason required by the text. For example, some people use manual line breaks to add space in a numbered list. There are much better ways to do this, so you should probably not consider this as a reason to avoid this step. Others use manual line breaks to create more logical line breaks in quoted material, including block quotes and verses or quotations used between the chapter title and the beginning of the chapter body text. In most of these cases, you will want to replace these with standard returns.

In rare cases, you may want to perform this Manual Line Break Replacement *after* the Global 3-step Return Replacement (Search #3, below). While scanning your document for manual line breaks (You did turn on "Show Invisibles," didn't you?), look for valid instances of double manual line breaks that might be removed by the Global 3-step Return Replacement. Double manual line breaks may be required by a multi-paragraph block quotation or a multi-verse poem. Alternatively, if the number of cases is small, you may decide to use this search as a selective replacement. On the other hand, if it is only a single passage, you will probably save more time by simply noting the chapter or chapters in which the double manual line breaks occur and restoring them after executing the global version of this replacement, and after performing replacement #3.

Reminder for selective replacements: first enter search terms; then, close Word's Find & Replace box and use **Cmd+G** (Apple) or **Ctrl+Alt+Y** (Windows) to "Find Again" (and again, and again, until the end). Caveat: Sometimes you will need to perform one search before closing the Find & Replace box, first.

## 3) Global 3-step Return Replacement

**Comment**: This replacement assures that your document will contain only single returns or double returns and takes three steps using placeholders. This replacement was briefly described in Chapter 3: "Introducing Search."

---

A. *Find what:* **^p^p**

   Replace All with: **%%** (This is the placeholder that I use; feel free to use another.)

B. *Find what:* **^p^p**

C. Replace All with **^p**

D. Repeat steps A and B until no more instances of **^p^p** are found

E. *Find what:* **%%**

F. *Replace with:* **^p^p** (Replace All)

---

## 4a) Global Space Before Paragraph Mark Replacement

**Comment**: This simple global search repairs situations in which you have typed a space immediately prior to typing a return. Such errors can happen for many reasons including typing very quickly. Remember the "Important Note" on page 36: where you see **space+** simply type a space and do not type the plus sign.

> A. *Find what:* **space+^p** *[a space character followed by a return (^p)]*
>
> *Replace with:* **^p** *[a single ^p]*
>
> B. Replace All and Repeat until no more instances of **space+return** are found

It will be necessary to have performed this search before doing the ellipsis repair searches in the following chapter.

## 4b) Global Paragraph Mark Followed by Space Replacement

**Comment**: This simple global search repairs situations in which you have typed a space immediately following typing a return. Such errors can happen for many reasons including typing very quickly. Another increasingly less common cause for this mistake is the typing of 2 to 5 spaces at the beginning of paragraphs, in place of an indent or a tab (tabs will be replaced by indents later in this chapter).

> A. *Find what:* **^p+space** *[a space character appearing after a return (^p)]*
>
> *Replace with:* **^p** *[a single ^p]*
>
> B. Replace All and repeat until no more instances of **return+space** are found

**Caution:** This search must be done before doing the paragraph capitalization repair search later in this chapter. Remember the "Important Note" on page 36: where you see **+space** simply type a space and do not type the plus sign.

## 5) Selective Paragraph Termination Search

**Comment**: This selective search targets paragraphs that do not close with punctuation and allows you to repair these as appropriate according to the context. A paragraph missing closing punctuation may require a period, exclamation mark, question mark, or quotation mark. You will need to make that determination on the fly. For this reason, the word "Replacement" is omitted from the name of this search.

A. With the cursor in the "Find what" field, select "Any letter" from the Special menu at the lower right of the fully expanded Find & Replace box. Then enter **^p**. The field should now contain **^$^p** (Alternatively you can simply type **^$^p** to achieve the same result).

B. Type a **period**+**^p** in the "Replace with" field. This is your default replacement text. Optionally, load this **period+return** into the clipboard. Because this is a selective replacement, you can override this at any time, simply by typing the necessary punctuation.

C. Close the Find & Replace box and repeatedly press **Cmd+G** (Apple) or **Ctrl+Alt+Y** (Windows) to "Find Again" (and again, and again). Each found chunk will be a paragraph missing terminating punctuation. Repair as needed, by pressing **Cmd+V** (Apple) or **Ctrl+V** (Windows) to replace the found text with the clipboard contents. But, before doing so, a right-arrow (possibly followed by a backspace) will be required so that the final letter of your paragraph is not deleted in the replacement (as part of the found text).

Depending up your version of Word, you may discover that it is necessary to click the "Find Next" button once before closing the Find & Replace box (otherwise the latest "Find what" field entry will not "take.")

Alternatively, leave the Find & Replace box open and manipulate the selective search from there, using the "Find Next" and "Replace" buttons being careful not to overwrite the last letter of the found text as described in the previous paragraph.

## 6) Global Tab Removal

**Comment**: Did you indent with a tab? Did you attempt to adjust the look of the page with a tab? You will find that using a true (ruler-based) indent or an indent within a Word style will serve you much better than using a tab.

Before removing all the tabs in your document, perform the following precautionary measures to compensate for instances of **space+tab** and **tab+space**. Any such combinations can lead to double spaces once you have removed all tabs, and therefore, need to be dealt with, first.

> A. *Find what:* **space+^t** *[space followed by tab]*
>
> B. *Replace with:* **space**
>
> C. Replace All
>
> D. Repeat, searching for **^t+space** *[tab followed by space]*

In case the **tab+space** or **space+tab** combination replacements have created instances of double spaces, quickly perform the #1 Global Double Space replacement to remedy the situation.

Now globally, replace all your tabs with nothing—the "Replace with" field will be empty. Make sure it is completely empty by tabbing into it and pressing the delete key.

> A. *Find what:* **^t** *[tab]*
>
>    *Replace with: [empty]*
>
> B. Replace All (press the Replace All button)

**Possible Problem:** In very rare cases, you may have unintentionally typed a tab when you meant to type a space. Performing this tab removal will have resulted in two words that were supposed to have a space between them now being run together.

**Solution:** Place the cursor at the beginning of your document and press **Opt+F7** (Apple) or **Alt+F7** (Windows) to jump to the next misspelled word, which might have been created by the previous tab removal, particularly if you ran a spell check before this final edit. You may repeat this until you reach the end of your manuscript.

Don't worry; when we assign styles to the body text, all the paragraphs will become indented again.

## Final Considerations for searches 4a, 4b, 5, and 6

The last four searches (#4a, #4b, #5, and #6) have taken care of unintentional spaces on either side of a return (paragraph mark or **^p**), paragraphs that are missing terminal punctuation, and unnecessary spaces appearing before and after tabs.

Your personal typing style may require that you search for a variety of strange punctuation pairings before your document is completely "clean" from a paragraphing point of view. For example, **tab+return (^t^p)** is a pattern that you may want to consider searching for before you go forward (replace with a single return). Others may have revealed themselves while you have monitored the previous four replacements (#4a, #4b, #5, and #6) during selective searches. These should be easy to spot because you have "Show Invisibles" enabled.

### 7) Selective Paragraph Capitalization Repair

**Comment**: All paragraphs should begin with a capital letter or an open quotation mark. If you use drop caps, Word may consider the paragraphs beginning with drop caps to have begun with a lowercase letter, but, if you read the "Common Mistakes" section of the "Basic Preparation" chapter, you will have been alerted to not use drop caps, just tell the book designer you'd like them. Because all paragraphs will, after a return, commence with a capital letter or an open quotation mark, we will use wildcards to search for cases that do not. You will need to repair each one individually; therefore, this repair cannot be done globally.

> A. Enable "Use wildcards"
>
> B. *Find what:* **[^13][!A-Z\"\\*\—^13]**
>
> C. Close the Find & Replace box and repeatedly press **Cmd+G (Apple)** or **Ctrl+Alt+Y** (Windows) to "Find Again" (and again, and again). Each found chunk will be a paragraph commencing with a lowercase letter or presenting some other mistake such as starting with a period or other disallowed punctuation. Repair as required.

**Explanation:** The first bracketed item in the "Find what" field is the ASCII character code for the **return** character. The next bracketed item commences with an **exclamation point**, indicating **NOT** to find any of the following characters or character ranges within the brackets. The remaining characters are first, the character range **A-Z** (meaning all capital letters); next the escaped characters: **open quotation mark** (because some paragraphs begin with an open quotation mark), an **asterisk** (for possible dingbats in hiatuses), and the **em dash** (for cases such as crediting the author of a quotation or endorsement on a new line). Remember, the "Important Note" on page 13: typing two hyphens will **not** automatically transform into an em dash inside the Find & Replace box; you must type **Shift+Opt+hyphen** (Mac) or **Alt+0151** (Windows). Note that you could have substituted **^147** for the **\"** as the first of the escaped characters if you find that approach easier. Last but not least is another **^13** for cases in which there are two returns in a row. Remember that our Search #3 likely left valid instances of double returns intact. The **NOT** expression following the initial return assures that none of these cases will be found.

All other cases are incorrect and include beginning paragraphs with lowercase letters or with incorrect punctuation or anything else not specified in the **NOT** expression. Fortunately, tab characters will not be included among these because we removed them earlier in this chapter; the indents will return when we assign styles to the paragraphs.

## 8) Selective Quoted Paragraph Second Character Repair

**Comment**: All paragraphs should begin with a capital letter or an open quotation mark, and we have made sure that is the case in the previous repair, but there is a possibility that paragraphs beginning with a quotation mark may (incorrectly) follow that quotation mark with a lowercase letter. The following selective search will allow you to repair any of these errors.

Remember, the "Important Note" on page 13: typing two hyphens will **not** automatically transform into an em dash inside the Find & Replace box; you must type **Shift+Opt+hyphen** (Mac) or **Alt+0151** (Windows). Likewise, typing three periods will **not** automatically transform into an ellipsis inside the Find & Replace box; you must type **Opt+semicolon** (Mac) or **Alt+0133** (Windows).

> A.   Enable "Use wildcards"
>
> B.   *Find what:* **[^13\"][!A-Z\—\...\.]**
>
> C.   Close the Find & Replace box and repeatedly press **Cmd+G** (Apple) or **Ctrl+Alt+Y** (Windows) to "Find Again" (and again, and again). Each found chunk will be a paragraph commencing with a lowercase letter or presenting some other mistake such as starting with a period or other disallowed punctuation. Repair as required.

**Explanation:** The first bracketed item in the "Find what" field is the ASCII character code for the return character followed by an escaped " for this (in other words \"); you can substitute **^147** (the ASCII character code for an open quotation mark), if you like. The next bracketed item commences with an **exclamation point**, indicating **NOT** to find any of the following: any characters in the range from capital **A** to capital **Z**, an escaped **em dash** (you could use **^151** for that), an escaped **ellipsis** character (you could substitute **^133** instead), and an escaped **period** for which you could substitute **^46**.

The period (**^46**) is in this group because you might have inadvertently typed it as the first of three dots making up an ellipsis. We will repair ellipses in the next chapter, so there is no reason to concern ourselves with those at this time.

The entire expression will find all paragraphs commencing with a quotation mark that is followed by a lowercase letter or incorrect punctuation mark.

**Variation**: Some writers start footnoted quotations with an asterisk preceding the open quotation mark instead of following the quotation. If you have done this, you should search for [^13\*] to repair those paragraphs.

### 9) Selective Sentence Capitalization Repair

**Comment**: Now that we have guaranteed that all paragraphs will begin correctly, we should give the same courtesy to sentences inside of paragraphs. To accomplish this, we search for all disallowed sentence *starts* that follow a proper sentence terminator that is followed by a single space. Thanks to the first search in this chapter, we do not have to worry that there might be cases of double spaces between sentences. It is likely that no errors of this kind will be found, but better to be safe than sorry.

---

A.   Enable "Use wildcards"

B.   *Find what:* [\.\?\!\—\…\"][^32][!A-Z\"]

   or [^46^63^151^133^148\!][^32][!A-Z^147]
   (See the explanation for using \!)

C.   Close the Find & Replace box and repeatedly press **Cmd+G** (Apple) or **Ctrl+Alt+Y** (Windows) to "Find Again" (and again, and again). Each found chunk will be a sentence commencing with a lowercase letter or presenting some other mistake such as starting with a period or other disallowed punctuation. Repair as required.

---

**Explanation**: If you have been reading the previous explanations, by now you should understand why there are two formats possible for the "Find what" field—one employs escaped characters to represent individual characters; the other uses ASCII character codes. On a Mac, it is not possible to use the character code ^33 inside the Find & Replace box hence, the escaped exclamation mark that it represents (\!).

## Reminder

Your self-editing will improve quickly using Word's Find and Replace options. For global searches, you can stay in the Find & Replace box and press the "Replace All" button. For selective replacements, first enter search terms (You may have to do the first search from within the box); then, close Word's Find & Replace box and use **Cmd+G** (Apple) or **Ctrl+Alt+Y** (Windows) to "Find Again" (and again, and again, until the end).

## Important Warnings

As noted within the searches in this chapter and also pertaining to all the searches in the following chapters, you must remember, the "Important Note" on page 13:

When you are inside the Find & Replace box, typing two hyphens will **not** automatically turn into an em dash as it does when you are typing in your document with the "Autocorrect symbols" preference enabled (see page 12); instead, you must type **Shift+Opt+hyphen** (Mac) or **Alt+0151** (Windows) to enter a true em dash in the "Find what" or "Replace with" fields. Alternatively, you can type **^+** to indicate an em dash in the Find & Replace box.

Likewise, typing three periods will **not** automatically turn into an ellipsis inside the Find & Replace box, as they do when you are typing in your document with the "Autocorrect symbols" preference enabled (see page 12); instead, you must type **Opt+semicolon** (Mac) or **Alt+0133** (Windows).

Consult the character tables on page 33 when you need to determine how to enter certain special characters into the Find & Replace box.

Keep in mind the "Important Note" on page 36 concerning spelled-out punctuation and plus signs.

Finally, you will encounter some searches that use an asterisk as a character (usually as an escaped character, meaning it has a backslash in front of it: \*); these are safe. However, when the asterisk is used as a symbol to represent any number of characters, problems may occur. In such cases, be very careful to monitor the search carefully. You would not want to inadvertently replace an entire chapter with a single em dash.

# Chapter Five

# Problematic Punctuation

## Search for Punctuation Problems

A great deal of punctuation errors can be repaired using *Final Edit* searches. For many of these, it will be necessary that you have at least enabled the "Replace as you type" in your Word Preferences so that "Straight quotation marks" will automatically be replaced by "smart quotation marks," and "Symbol characters (--) by symbols (—)." Automatic replacement of symbol characters deals with more than just em dashes: ellipses, when expressed as three periods, are also converted to a single ellipsis character.

We will start with the simplest of punctuation: three sentence terminators: the period, question mark, and exclamation mark, and initially deal with these on the simplest level to ensure that there is never a space before a sentence terminator.

---

"A perfectly healthy sentence, it is true, is extremely rare. For the most part we miss the hue and fragrance of the thought; as if we could be satisfied with the dews of the morning or evening without their colors, or the heavens without their azure."                              —Henry David Thoreau

---

## 10a) Global Sentence Terminator Repair

**Comment:** This one is simple. We will search for a space followed by a period, question mark, or exclamation mark, and then remove the space. We could do this as three separate searches for 1) **space+period**, 2) **space+question** mark, and 3) **space+ exclamation mark**, but we can also accomplish this in a single step using wildcards. Ellipses, em dashes, and quotation marks can also terminate sentences, and those will be covered later in the chapter.

> A.   Enable "Use wildcards"
>
> B.   *Find what:* **([^32])([^46\?\!])**
>
>      *Replace with:* **\2**
>
> C.   Press the Replace All button. Repeat until zero cases are found.

**Explanation of Find what:** The first expression contains the bracketed ASCII code for the space character (**^32**), meaning that the space must occur. The second expression contains the bracketed representations of a period, question mark, and exclamation mark: **^46\?\!** (The question mark and exclamation mark must be expressed as escaped characters by preceding them with a backslash. On a Mac—by the way, I am using a Mac—using the ASCII codes results in an error for either of these characters). The search will find any of the three characters in this expression.

**Explanation of Replace with:** The **\2** replaces the found chunk with the second expression in the "Find what" field. Expressions are enclosed in parentheses. The second one will contain whichever character was found following a space, therefore, by omitting the first expression, **\1**, the punctuation mark will appear without the space.

## 10b) Global Phrase and Clause Punctuation Repair

**Comment:** This is another simple replacement. We will search for a space followed by a semi-colon, colon, or comma, and then remove the space. We could do this as three searches for 1) space+semi-colon, 2) space+colon, and 3) space+comma, but we can also accomplish this in a single step using wildcards. Ellipses, em dashes, and quotation marks can also follow phrases and clauses, but those will be dealt with later in this chapter.

| | |
|---|---|
| A. | Enable "Use wildcards" |
| B. | *Find what:* ([^32])([^58^59^44]) |
| | *Replace with:* \2 |
| C. | Press the Replace All button |

**Explanation:** See the explanations that follow the previous replacement. The same principles apply here.

## 10c) Global Sentence, Phrase, and Clause Punctuation Repair (combined)

**Comment:** This search combines the two previous ones into a single replacement. It is not a separate search, and if you have completed the two previous searches, you should not perform this one. However, in the future, you may wish to use this combined form.

The searches were presented in this way to help you understand the power of wildcards to make your searches do double duty (actually, they can do much more) and thereby, cut your search time in half (or more).

| | |
|---|---|
| A. | Enable "Use wildcards" |
| B. | *Find what:* ([^32])([^46\?\!^58^59^44]) |
| | *Replace with:* \2 |
| C. | Press the Replace All button |

As this replacement shows, the flexibility of wildcards can save you a great deal of time. Consider the steps you would have had to go through to complete the search above without wildcards:

## The Inefficiency of Search 10c *Without* using Wildcards

| Action | Find what: | Replace with: |
|---|---|---|
| Replace all | space+period | period |
| Replace all | space+question mark | question mark |
| Replace all | space+exclamation mark | exclamation mark |
| Replace all | Space+semi-colon | semi-colon |
| Replace all | space+colon | colon |
| Replace all | space+comma | comma |

For Macintosh users, the use of wildcards may be all the more scary. Window users long have been forced to type character codes for such things as em dashes, en dashes, ellipses, bullets, and even curly quotes. They are used to it. On the other hand, Mac users have always had these and more than a hundred other characters available to them, directly, through keystroke combinations that are both logically placed and easy to remember.

### 11a) Global Straight to Curly Quotes Replacement (normal)

**Comment:** If you have used either the straight single quote or straight double quote to indicate inches or feet, then you will need to follow this search with the next one.

A. *Find what:* [single quote character]
   (type a single quote character into *Find what:*)

   *Replace with:* [single quote character]
   (type a single quote character into *Replace with:*)

B. Press the Replace All button

C. *Find what:* [double quote character]
   (type a double quote character into *Find what:*)

   *Replace with:* [double quote character]
   (type a double quote character into *Replace with:*)

D. Press the Replace All button

By replacing the quote characters with another copy of themselves (now that you have enabled the Word Preference to replace "Straight quotations marks" with "smart quotation marks") Word will automatically repair them, making the correct determination for each one according to whether or not an **open quotation mark** or a **close quotation mark** is required. As a bonus, the above search will take care of apostrophes, too.

## 11b) Global or Selective Restoration of Inches and/or Feet

**Comment:** This search will restore your inches and feet (single and double straight quotes) that may have been inadvertently converted to curly quotes by the previous search.

This search will take care of your inches and feet passages with or without a space between your foot sign (single straight quote) and the number following that bears the inches sign (double straight quote). Because this search includes an asterisk (*) to indicate any number of characters, you should probably not perform it as a global replacement.

---

A.  Enable "Use wildcards"

B.  *Find what:* **([0-9])(')(*[0-9]*)(")**

  *Replace with:* **\1^039\3^034**

C.  Use Selective Replacement (Choose "Find Next" or "Replace" as required)

  You don't really need to understand why this works, but if you'd like to, so you can come up with complex searches on your own, read the next two paragraphs.

---

**Explanation of Find what:** The first parenthesized item of the "Find what" field is the "number in range" command: the bracketed **0-9** (zero to nine). This looks for any digit in that range; in other words, any digit. The second parenthesized item is a curly single **close quotation mark** (type **shift+opt+]** on a Mac). The third parenthesized item is **asterisk**, meaning any character, including the space character, or no character whatsoever. This is in case you put space between some cases of inches and feet but omitted that in other cases. The **asterisk** is followed by the number in range indicator: the bracketed **0-9**. This is followed by another **asterisk** to account for the possibility of double-digit inches such as 10 or 11 inches. The Fourth parenthesized item is a curly double **close quotation mark** (type **shift+opt+[** on a Mac).

**Explanation of Replace with:** The **\1** retains the first parenthesized item. The **^039** is the ASCII character number of the single straight quote, and this will be substituted for the existing curly single quote. The **\3** retains the third parenthesized item, which may be a single digit or a double digit, and may be preceded by a space. The **^034** is the ASCII character number for a straight double quote, and this will be substituted for the existing curly double quote.

**Caution:** This search can yield false positives. To reduce false positives, omit the second asterisk if you have no 2-digit inches.

## 12a) Global Multi-Stage Em Dash Replacement (Preliminary)

**Comment:** Besides using em dashes to offset appositive phrases or to indicate interruptions in dialogue, in fiction writing, use em dashes instead of parentheses. Em dashes are the longest dashes available; they are the same width of that of a capital letter "M" in the prevailing typeface. To make sure you have not used parentheses and convert any you have used to em dashes, perform the following searches.

---

A.   Enable "Use wildcards"

B.   *Find what:* **[\(\)]**

   *Replace with:* **^+**

C.   Replace All or use Selective Replacement if you have valid parentheses.

---

**Explanation:** We need to use a backslash \ before the left-parenthesis, as well as the right-parenthesis, because this replacement has wildcards enabled, and parentheses have another function with wildcards enabled—they indicate expressions. The escape character (**backslash**) tells Word to treat the character that follows as a character and not part of an expression. Note that **^+** is the symbol that Word uses to represent em dashes.

## 12b) Global Multi-Stage Em Dash Replacement (Main Operation)

**Comment:** For this search to work effectively, you must enable the automatic conversion of two dashes to a true em dash in the "Auto Correct" option of Word's Preferences. Searching for two hyphens and replacing them with two hyphens while the Auto Correct option is enabled will convert them to true em dashes.

| |
|---|
| A. *Find what:* **--** [two hyphens]<br><br>*Replace with:* **--** *[two hyphens, alternatively, an em dash:* **shift-option-hyphen***]* |
| B. Replace All |

In case you accidentally typed three hyphens, or more, in place of an em dash, you should perform the following precautionary searches after the main search, above. Em dashes always butt up against the words they separate, without any spaces. In fact the only punctuation that can precede an em dash is a return or an open quotation mark. And, the only character that can follow an em dash besides a letter is a close quotation mark or a return.

## 12c) Global Multi-Stage Em Dash Replacement (Precautionary)

| Action | Find what: | Replace with: |
|---|---|---|
| Replace all, Repeat until zero | space+hyphen+space | em dash |
| Replace all, Repeat until zero | space+en dash+space | em dash |
| Replace all, Repeat until zero | hyphen+em dash | em dash |
| Replace all, Repeat until zero | em dash+hyphen | em dash |
| Replace all, Repeat until zero | space+em dash | em dash |
| Replace all, Repeat until zero | em dash+space | em dash |
| Replace all, Repeat until zero | em dash+em dash | em dash |

We will use this Precautionary Replacements format, or portions thereof, when dealing with most punctuation errors on a global level. Remember the "Important Note" on page 36 concerning the spelled-out punctuation used in conjunction with the plus sign.

### 13a) Global Multi-Stage Ellipsis Replacement

**Comment**: Remember to enable the automatic conversion of two dashes to a true em dash in the "Auto Correct" option of Word's Preferences. The precise wording of this preference is "Symbol characters (--) with symbols (—)" but it covers ellipses, too. Searching for three periods, and replacing with three periods while this option is enabled will convert them to true ellipses.

> A.  *Find what: ... [three periods]*
>
> *Replace with:  ...  [three periods, alternatively, an ellipsis character: option semi-colon or* **alt+0133**]
>
> B.  Replace All

If your frequency of typos requires it, you should perform the following precautionary searches, too.

### 13b) Global Multi-Stage Ellipsis Replacement (Precautionary)

| Action | Find what: | Replace with: |
|---|---|---|
| Replace all, Repeat until zero | ellipsis+ellipsis | ellipsis |
| Replace all, Repeat until zero | ellipsis+period+period | period+ellipsis |
| Replace all, Repeat until zero | period+period+ellipsis | period+ellipsis |
| **Your writing may require the following to be a selective searches** | | |
| Replace all, Repeat until zero | four periods | period+ellipsis or an ellipsis |
| Replace all, Repeat until zero | five periods | period+ellipsis |

## 13c) Selective Multi-Stage Ellipsis Replacement (Special Cases)

| Action | Find what: | Possibility: |
|---|---|---|
| Depending upon whether omitted material is before or after ellipsis | | |
| Replace all, Repeat until zero | ellipsis+? | ?+ellipsis |
| Replace all, Repeat until zero | ?+ellipsis | ellipsis+? |
| Replace all, Repeat until zero | ellipsis+! | !+ellipsis |
| Replace all, Repeat until zero | !+ellipsis | ellipsis+! |
| Replace all, Repeat until zero | ellipsis+comma | comma+ellipsis |
| Replace all, Repeat until zero | comma+ellipsis | ellipsis+comma |

## En Dashes

For many writers, the en dash is a mystery. But if you take care of this elusive item, you will save much time and money in the book-design stage, as well as sending a subtle signal to those who read your book, including agents and publishers, that you are not a novice.

En dashes are the second longest dashes available; they are the same width as that of a capital letter "N" in the prevailing typeface. En dashes are longer than a hyphen but shorter than an em dash. On a Mac, type **option+hyphen** for an en dash; on Windows, type **Alt 0150**. For more Windows character codes, see "How to Type Special Characters" at the end of Chapter 3.

Many people confuse hyphens with en dashes. The primary use of the en dash is between an inclusive range of numbers. This includes dates, times, and any ranges of numbers such as page numbers. With en dashes' affinity to numbers expressing times and dates, it will come as no surprise that ranges of days use en dashes, too (Monday–Wednesday), as do seasons (Spring–Summer schedule). En dashes should not be used when *from* or *between* appears before any of the phrases that would otherwise require an en dash; instead, substitute *to* for the en dash. Use en dashes to express open-ended dates such as the life span of someone who is still alive. On the other side of a number, use en dashes as minus signs, if you have incorrectly used hyphens for negative numbers.

Use en dashes for nouns that require linking that would render a hyphen incorrect; for example, Parent–Teacher Association.

In some ways the en dash can serve as a "super-hyphen" in the same way that a semi-colon can serve as a "super-comma." For example: the Asheville–Winston-Salem bus (note that Winston-Salem is hyphenated, but an en dash appears between Asheville and Winston-Salem). Non-hyphenated multi-word adjectives often take en dashes when connected to another word, suffix, or prefix: He took a pre–Thanksgiving holiday, New York–Miami flight. Both of the dashes are en dashes.

Travel destinations and other place names offer many examples of en dash usage. This example highlights the difference between hyphens and en dashes: She spoke Swiss-German (hyphen), and lived close to the Swiss–German border (en dash).

The complexities of en dash usage mean that most global replacements are difficult and many cases require individual scrutiny. Once I edited a 135,000-word manuscript in which the author had used single hyphens in place of all dashes—em dashes, en dashes, and hyphens. With the exception of the replacements below, I had to search for and examine every hyphen in the manuscript. Fortunately, you have the advantage of at least having taken care of your em dashes by way of the previous replacement. That will reduce your need for selective searches considerably. Another thing that will reduce the amount of time required by en dashes is that presumably, you are the author of the manuscript upon which you are executing this final edit. If you have hyphenated any of the cases that should be en dashes, you will know that from the start and be able to search directly for those cases.

Considering what you now know about en dashes, you can correctly assume that any mass correction of en dashes in your manuscript will end up saving you much time, and if you plan to hire an editor or book designer, their tasks will be greatly simplified, and, consequently, less time-consuming and less expensive.

## 14a) Global En Dash Replacement (Numeric Ranges)

**Comment**: The most common use of en dashes is between numbers. The following replacement will take care of such instances, globally, although you may want to perform this as a selective replacement if you are aware that your manuscript has special cases that require hyphens. Alternatively, you may want to perform this global replacement and afterwards, search for your exceptions individually, particularly if you have a larger number of required replacements than exceptions.

> A. Enable "Use wildcards"
>
> B. *Find what:* **([0-9])(-)([0-9])** *[Note: The character in the central expression is a hyphen]*
>
> *Replace with:* **\1–\3** *[Note: The middle character is an en dash]* or **\1^=\3** *[Note: ^= represents an en dash]*
>
> C. Replace All or use Selective Replacement if your manuscript has exceptions.

**Explanation:** All hyphens between any two numbers are replaced with an en dash. For the "Replace with" field, you may use **^=** to represent the en dash. That is the entity that Word will place in the field if you select "en dash" from the Special popup menu while in the "Replace with" field while "Use wildcards" is enabled.

## 14b) Optional Global En Dash Replacement (Negative Numbers)

**Comment**: The minus sign indicating a negative number should not be a hyphen; it should be an en dash. Skip this search if you know that your manuscript contains no negative numbers.

> A. Enable "Use wildcards"
>
> B. *Find what:* **(^32)(-)([0-9])**
>
> *Replace with:* **\1–\3**  or  **\1^=\3**
>
> C. Replace All or use Selective Replacement if your manuscript has exceptions.

**Explanation:** All hyphens between a space and a number are replaced with an en dash.

## 14c) Optional Global En Dash Replacement (Days of the Week)

**Comment**: Ranges of days should be separated by en dashes. You may skip this replacement if you know that your manuscript contains no such patterns.

> A.  Enable "Use wildcards"
>
> B.  *Find what:* **(?day)(-)([MTWFS])**
>
>     *Replace with:* **\1–\3**  or  **\1^=\3**
>
> C.  Replace All or use Selective Replacement if your manuscript has exceptions.

**Explanation:** All hyphens between a word ending in "**day**" and a word beginning with a capital **M, T, W, F,** or **S** are replaced with an en dash. All days of the week commence with one of those five letters and end with "day."

## 14d) Optional Selective En Dash Replacement (Ranges of Months)

**Comment**: Ranges of months should be separated by en dashes. Skip this search if you know that your manuscript contains no such patterns. Resist the temptation to perform this as a global replacement for the reasons stated in the explanation, below.

> A.  Enable "Use wildcards"
>
> B.  *Find what:* **([yhletr])(-)([JFMASOND])**
>
>     *Replace with:* **\1–\3**
>
> C.  Perform a selective replacement, pressing Find Next or Replace as appropriate.

**Explanation:** All hyphens between a word ending in **y, h, l, e, t,** or **r** and a word beginning with a capital **J, F, M, A, S, O, N,** or **D** are replaced with an en dash. These correspond to all the possible first and last letters of the names of the months. This search is a selective replacement because it will also pick up valid hyphens such as the one in Haight-Ashbury.

## 14e) Optional Selective En Dash Replacement (Most Others)

**Comment**: By performing the first four en dash replacements, you will have greatly reduced the number of incorrect hyphens in your document. Most, but not all, correct hyphens appear between two lowercase letters. Many, but not all, en dashes occurring between two words will have the second word capitalized. This search will find all hyphenations between a word ending in a lowercase letter and one beginning with an uppercase letter.

A. Enable "Use wildcards"

B. *Find what:* **([a-z])(-)([A-Z])**

    *Replace with:* **\1–\3** or **\1 ^=\3**

C. Perform a selective replacement, pressing Find Next or Replace as appropriate.

## 14f) Optional Selective En Dash Replacement (The Rest)

**Variation:** If you have performed most or all of the en dash replacements, and you have some time left at the conclusion of your final edit, you may want to substitute **([a-Z])(-)([a-z])** for the search expression in the previous search. This will find hyphens between words ending in a lowercase letter and ones beginning with a lowercase letter, as well as between words ending with an uppercase letter and ones beginning with a lowercase letter.

Alternatively, you may want to simply selectively search for all hyphens for inspection and correction as required. The number of times you have to do the find operation will have been greatly reduced by the en dash replacements you have already accomplished.

## *Quotation marks*

When we talk about problems with quotation marks, we are primarily concerned with other punctuation in combination with the close quotation mark. The quotation mark rules are very simple, but many writers are unaware of those rules. Periods and commas are *always* placed inside the close quotation mark; rare exceptions exist. Question marks and exclamation marks can appear on either side of the close quotation mark; usually the correct position is obvious, but sometimes this is not the case. Fortunately, semicolons and colons are *always* placed outside the close quotation mark. The use of quotation marks is easier to understand when all the usages are lined up on a table such as the one on the next page.

| Close quotation mark plus | Location (Inside) | Location (Outside) |
|---|---|---|
| Period | Inside: ." | If followed by a citation in parentheses, omit period and place after parentheses. |
| Comma | Inside ," | |
| Semicolon | | Outside "; |
| Colon | | Outside ": |
| Question mark | Inside if the mark pertains to the quoted material, or if both the quoted material and the entire sentence would have the mark. | Outside if the mark pertains to the entire sentence. |
| Exclamation mark | Inside if the mark pertains to the quoted material, or if both the quoted material and the entire sentence would have the mark. | Outside if the mark pertains to the entire sentence. |
| Em dash | Inside if the mark pertains to the quoted material, or if both the quoted material and the entire sentence would have the mark. | Outside if the mark pertains to the entire sentence. |
| Ellipsis | Inside if the mark pertains to the quoted material, or if both the quoted material and the entire sentence would have the mark. | Outside if the mark pertains to the entire sentence. |

## 15a) Global Quote Plus Period or Comma Transposition

**Comment**: This replacement looks for any commas or periods that fall outside of a close quotation mark and moves them inside the close quotation mark. For optimal results, you must have executed replacements 10a, 10b, and 10c before this replacement and the ones that follow.

> A. Enable "Use wildcards"
>
> B. *Find what:* (**[\"])([^46^44])**
>
>    *Replace with:* **\2\1**
>
> C. Press Replace All.

**Explanation:** The first expression in the "Find what" field is an escaped **close quotation mark**. The second expression succeeds if either a period (**^46**) or a comma (**^44**) follows. The "Replace with" field (**\2\1**) reverses the order of these elements. "Replace All" transposes the order of all occurrences of this pattern.

## 15b) Optional Selective Parenthesized Citation Repair

**Comment:** The one exception to the above transposition occurs when a Modern Language Association (MLA) formatted citation appears in parentheses following the quoted material. If your manuscript contains such a pattern, then perform the following replacement and move the period. Because this search contains an asterisk, remember the Warnings on page 46.

> A. Enable "Use wildcards"
>
> B. *Find what:* (**[^46])([\"])([^32])([^40])(\*)([^41]**)
>
>    *Replace with:* **\2\3\4\5\6\1**
>
> C. Perform a selective replacement, pressing Find Next or Replace as appropriate.

**Explanation:** The "Find what" field contains six expressions specifying of a period followed by a close quotation mark, then a space followed by a left parenthesis, followed by any number of characters (**\***) followed by a right parenthesis. The "Replace with" changes the order of these expressions so that the first one (the period) appears last.

## 15c) Global Quote Plus Semicolon or Colon Transposition

**Comment**: This search looks for any semicolons or colons that fall inside of a close quotation mark and moves them outside the close quotation mark. For optimal results, you must have executed searches 10a, 10b, and 10c before this one and the ones that follow.

> A.  Enable "Use wildcards"
>
> B.  *Find what:* ([\;\:])([\"])
>
>     *Replace with:* \2\1
>
> C.  Press Replace All.

**Explanation**: The first expression in the "Find what" field contains an escaped **semicolon** and an escaped **colon**. The second expression is an escaped **close quotation mark**. Replace All transposes the order of all occurrences of this pattern.

## 15d.1) Selective 3-Step Quote + Punctuation Transposition (Step 1)

Remember the chart several pages back? Question marks, exclamation marks, ellipses, and em dashes can appear on either side of a close quotation mark. You may have written your book with a partial understanding of the rules. Perform this search as Step 1, 2 and 3 only if you have the rules completely backward. You may want to omit Step 2 (see possible reasons in its comment).

**Comment**: This search looks for any question marks, exclamation marks, ellipses, or em dashes that fall outside of a close quotation mark and selectively moves them inside the close quotation mark. For optimal results, you must have executed searches 10a, 10b, and 10c before this one and the ones that follow.

> A.  Enable "Use wildcards"
>
> B.  *Find what:* ([\"])([\?\!\...\—])
>
>     *Replace with:* \2^37\1 [Note: This inserts a percent sign as a placeholder.]
>
> C.  Use Slective Transposition as required.

**Explanation:** The first expression in the "Find what" field is an escaped close quotation mark. The second expression will succeed if any of the escaped characters follows: **question mark, exclamation mark, ellipsis,** or **em dash.** The "Replace with" field (**\2\1**) reverses the order of these elements if you press the Replace button or finds the next occurrence if you press the Find Next button. Because this is a three-stage transposition, a placeholder percent sign (**^37**) is inserted between the two elements.

## 15d.2) Selective 3-Step Quote After Punctuation Transpose (Step 2)

This search is optional. If you truly have the rules backward, as suggested in Step 1 of this search, then you should perform this step. If your knowledge of the rules concerning placing punctuation inside the closing quotation mark is more complete than the rules governing placing punctuation outside the closing quotation mark (this is much more often the case than the reverse), then you might not need to perform this Step of the search. Instead, proceed directly to Step 3.

**Comment**: This search looks for any question marks, exclamation marks, ellipses, or em dashes that fall inside of a close quotation mark and selectively moves them outside the close quotation mark. For optimal results, you must have executed searches 10a, 10b, and 10c before this search and the ones that follow. The placeholder percent sign, inserted in stage one of this three-stage transposition assures that replacements performed in stage one will be ignored by this search.

> A.   Enable "Use wildcards"
>
> B.   Find what: (**[\?\!\...\—])([\"])**
>
> Replace with: **\2\1**
>
> C.   Use Slective Transposition as required.

**Explanation:** The first expression in the "Find what" field succeeds if any of the escaped characters: **question mark, exclamation mark, ellipsis,** or **em dash** precedes the second expression, an escaped **close quotation mark**. The "Replace with" field (\2\1) reverses the order of these elements if you press the Replace button or finds the next occurrence if you press the Find Next button.

### 15d.3) Global 3-Step Quote After Punctuation Transposition (Step 3)

**Comment**: Now you must remove all the placeholders inserted by the initial part of this three-stage transposition. This can be accomplished by the following global search.

---

A.  Enable "Use wildcards"

B.  *Find what:* (\[\?\!\!\...\—])(\[^37])(\[\"])

    *Replace with:* \1\3

C.  Press Replace All.

---

# Chapter Six

# Dealing with Dialogue

## Jack said, Jill said, He said, She said

*If your manuscript does not contain dialogue, you can skip this chapter until you write a book that requires it.*

The proper use of dialogue can vouchsafe the success or failure of a book. Unfortunately, many misconceptions about dialogue eventually find their way into published material and this leads to the widespread distribution of dialogue myths. Violators of immutable dialogue laws point to such publications as justification of their crimes. The greatest problems arise through the misuse of dialogue attributions.

Dialogue attributions identify the person voicing the lines of dialogue to which they refer. Dialogue attributions consist either of a tagline or an action beat or both.

Taglines, sometimes referred to as dialogue tags or simply, tags, take the form *Character name + verb indicating the manner of speaking (e.g. said or asked)*. A pronoun may substitute for the character name. The speaking verb always appears *after* the character name or pronoun (extremely rare exceptions will be mentioned later in this chapter). Taglines that include speaking verbs are never connected to their dialogue line by a period, the most common connection being a comma placed either inside the close quotation mark that precedes the tagline or following the tagline that precedes the dialogue. When dialogue or a portion of a line of dialogue precedes its attribution, question marks and exclamation marks are permitted (inside the close quotation mark); semicolons, dashes, and ellipses are not. To endow a dialogue line with greater significance than other dialogue lines, a colon may connect the tagline to the dialogue line, but only when the tagline precedes the dialogue line and only when the dialogue line is an uninterrupted complete sentence containing an independent clause with a subject and a verb.

Action beats, sometimes referred to simply as beats, identify the character speaking through action rather than by using a speaking verb. Because of their proximity to the dialogue line, we assume such beats imply that the character whose action is described in the beat is the same character speaking the dialogue line that precedes or follows the beat. Beats are always separated from their associated dialogue lines with terminal punctuation; commas and semicolons are not permitted. Sometimes, a beat is combined with a tagline, either in the same sentence or as a separate sentence. In such combinations, the tagline element is always closest to the actual dialogue line.

Two serious misconceptions are often presented by clueless writing instructors and self-proclaimed grammar gurus in their blogs or other instructional treatises, now globally available, thanks to the Internet.

The first misconception is that the speaking verb (said, asked, shouted, etc.) is allowed to come before the character name or pronoun doing the speaking: "said she" instead of "she said."

The inverted form in which the verb precedes the speaker (e.g. *said Jack*) is not permitted unless certain very strict conditions prevail, and this reversal will *never* be found in the work of serious writers except in those extremely rare cases that permit the rule to be broken. Within writing that actually sells, including all bestsellers, less than 1% of the attributions will be in the inverted pattern. The exceptions themselves are complicated to explain and to communicate to novice writers, particularly when those writers are overwhelmed with misinformation to the contrary. Again, a study of bestsellers using corpus linguistic software such as FictionFixer clearly reveals the absolute falsehood of any claims that deny the dialogue maxims in this chapter. Data from FictionFixer establishes, beyond any doubts, what dialogue forms are practiced by the world's most best selling professional writers.

1) Exceptions due to the speaker reference being long enough to position the verb too far away from the dialogue. An article or a possessive pronoun almost always precedes such cases.

**Article "a":** "Excuse me," said a tall blonde man with one black shoe.

**Article "the":** "With pleasure," said the woman wearing the leopard-skin pillbox hat.

**Possessive "her":** "More cake please," said her uncle from the Pacific Northwest.

**Possessive "their":** "Not today," said their third nanny in almost as many months.

2) Exceptions for reasons of clarity, particularly when reading the passage aloud could cause confusion of meaning.

"I'll donate twenty percent of the profit, too," said Chief Justice McPherson.

In this last case, if the "said" were to follow the speaker and the passage were to be read aloud, this could be heard as *I'll donate twenty percent of the profit to Chief Justice McPherson* long before the verb "said" is encountered. Upon reaching the trailing verb, the listener is forced to reinterpret the entire sentence that preceded it, and that misinterpreted sentence itself may have already triggered a reinterpretation of everything that has transpired so far in the story. By the time the listener has straightened things out and reassigned the correct interpretation of everything affected, he has missed the next three or four sentences and is now hopelessly lost. The same can happen to a rapid silent reader, or someone who simply doesn't read very closely. A "speed-bump" of this magnitude can trigger aftershocks throughout one's story. The professional writer will realize that a sentence–attribution combination with such inherent destructive potential requires a momentary suspension of the rules.

The second popular misconception is that writers should avoid "said" as much as possible and, in its place, substitute any sound-related term imaginable, the more obscure, the more desirable. I have seen novels in which the author did not use "said" even once because of this misconception, to the detriment of the work. Because I work in the field of computational linguistics using the corpus of bestselling novels for my research, I can state with certainty that this does not occur in books by bestselling authors.

To promote either of these misconceptions is tantamount to a music teacher promoting the notion that a performance should include wrong notes "in order to distinguish one's performance from that of others performing the same work," and the more wrong notes, the merrier!

The truth of the matter is that 80% or more of your attributions should use the verbs "said" or "asked." "Said" is always *invisible* to the reader and "asked" shares that characteristic in most cases. The remaining 20% of attributions should be distributed among words that can actually refer to human speech! In other words, you cannot say, "she grinned" or "she grimaced" in place of "she said" because grinning and grimacing cannot produce human words.

Use "said" more than all the other attributions combined: at least twice as often as "asked." The complete list of acceptable attributions follows, in order of preference by frequency of usage by bestselling authors (determined by FictionFixer).

**NORMAL:** *said, asked*

**EXOTIC:** *insisted, shouted, answered, whispered, gasped, explained, demanded, cried, responded, lied, observed, murmured, stuttered, mumbled, snarled, screamed, protested, muttered, hissed, yelled, replied, groaned, begged, added, declared, confessed, railed, pleaded, conceded, whined, pointed out,* and *"signed"* (if a character uses sign language)

You will notice that every verb on the list can actually refer to the act of human speech. In this text, we will use the term "exotic" to refer to all attribution verbs that are not "said" or "asked."

You may be wondering why "thought" is not on this list. Do not consider "thought" to be a dialogue attribution verb, rather, it is a thought attribution verb (like *pondered, contemplated, reflected, speculated,* and *imagined*). Thoughts may, in rare instances, require attributions, but the thoughts, themselves, are usually not placed in quotes. Thoughts may be in italics or not, but italicized "thoughts" do not require an attribution verb.

Later in this chapter, you will learn some searches that will enable you to calculate the frequency of your dialogue attributions.

# Dialogue Repair

Because the overwhelming majority of your attribution verbs should be "said," the initial dialogue repair searches will be concerned with that verb. First we will run several selective precautionary searches in preparation—cases in which "Said" is capitalized and cases in which a closing quotation mark is missing before the "said." Next, we will perform four or five global transpositions. The first two will repair all cases of "said" appearing before a capitalized one- or two-word character name. An optional third search covers cases in which one or more of your characters has a title (Dr., Mrs., Rev., Maj., etc.). The next two will repair all cases of "said" preceding the pronouns "he" or "she." Trailing punctuation, if any, will be retained in all transpositions. Then, we will run a selective precautionary search for cases in which the speaker is not capitalized; for example, "said the man in the dark blue suit." Finally, we will examine and repair incorrectly inverted forms of other attribution verbs.

## 16) Selective Capitalized "Said" Inspection and Repair

**Comment:** The acceptable cases of a capitalized "Said" are so few that your selective search should be quite brief. Note: this means that the initial 'S' is capitalized, not the entire word.

| |
|---|
| A.  Disable "Use wildcards" and Enable "Match case" |
| B.  *Find what:* **Said** |
|     *Replace with:* **said** |
| C.  Use Selective Replacement (Choose "Find Next" or "Replace" as required) |

**Explanation:** "Match case" ensures that the search only finds capitalized instances of the word "Said." Keeping the lowercase version in the "Replace with" field means you need only press the "Replace" button to replace the found text and jump to the next instance, or the "Find Next" button to proceed to the next instance without changing a capitalized "Said" that does not require alteration.

## 17) Selective "Said" with Missing Quotation Mark (Precautionary)

**Comment:** Nearly all cases of the word "said" (lowercased) will be preceded by a close quotation mark. This precautionary search allows you to quickly target and repair those, adding a close quotation mark with the simple press of the "Replace" button. You may be tempted to repair the leading "said" that follows the now-corrected punctuation, but you will probably save more time by using the next three searches to accomplish that task.

> A.  Enable "Use wildcards"
>
> B.  *Find what:* **([\?\!.,'—…])(^32)(said)**
>
>     *Replace with:* **\1"\2\3**
>
> C.  Use Selective Replacement (Choose "Find Next" or "Replace" as required)

**Explanation:** The "Find what" field contains the escaped characters question mark and exclamation mark, followed by **period, comma, close single quotation mark (apostrophe), em dash,** and **ellipsis.** This is followed by a **space** and the word **said** (uncapitalized). The "Replace with" field retains these three items (one of the five punctuation signs in the first expression, the space, and the word "said") in the same order but inserts a **close double quotation mark** between expressions 1 and 2, in other words, between the punctuation and the space. Simply press "Find Next" if the found text does not include an error, meaning it can stand without the inserted close double quotation mark.

## 18a) Global or Selective "Said" with One-Word Character Name

**Comment:** If you have used one-word character names in your attributions, and you want to globally transpose any instances that might have a "said" preceding the character name, Word makes it very simple. You can do these with two global searches. On the other hand, if you have used titles with a character's last name; for example, Dr. Smith, Mrs. Peacock, or Maj. Robertson, you will need to run this first transposition as a selective search, because the only logical manner in which to design this search requires allowing the possibility that the end of any one-word character name might be a terminal punctuator such as a period. Therefore, when done globally, the search would assume "Dr." or "Mrs." or any other abbreviated title ending in period to be the entire character name. Similarly, if you have used any two-word character names, the search must be run selectively, otherwise, the "said" might be inserted between the two words of the character name.

**The solution:** if you have used titles for any of your characters in dialogue attributions, or if you have used two-word character names in your dialogue attributions, you must run this search as a selective transposition, otherwise, perform the search as a global transposition.

Alternatively, if you are confident that you have used the two-word forms a greater number of times than the one-word forms, you may want to first perform the search that follows this one, and then return and do this search after having taken care of all the two-word character name attributions.

> A. Enable "Use wildcards"
>
> B. *Find what:* **([\?\!.,' — ...])(" ^32)(said)(^32)¬ (<[A-Z]\*[a-z]>)([!][A-z])**
>
> *Replace with:* **\1\2\5\4\3\6**
>
> C. Use Global or Selective Transposition (See the comment for which one to use), but be careful if you go Global because of the asterisk. You may want to read the warning on page 46.

**Explanation:** The "Find what" field contains six expressions. The first includes all the terminators you might find preceding the close quotation mark in dialogue preceding an attribution. The second expression is the **close quotation mark** followed by a **space**. The third expression is the word **said** in lowercase (you already fixed any incorrectly capitalized instances of "Said" with the first search in this chapter). The fourth expression represents a **space** (^32). The fifth expression is a word that begins with a capital letter and ends with a lowercase letter and has any number of characters in between. The sixth expression is any character that is not a letter. The "Replace with" field re-orders these elements correctly, as indicated by the numbers preceded by backslashes.

## 18b) Selective "Said" with Two-Word Character Name

**Comment:** You can skip this if you have not used any of your characters' full two-word names in dialogue attributions, but don't skip it if you have used titles with a character's last name; for example, Dr. Smith, Mrs. Peacock, or Maj. Robertson. If you have used two-word character names, or titles (abbreviated or unabbreviated) followed by a singe word character name, then this transposition will move the "said" from the incorrect position of preceding the two-word name to the correct position—that of following the two-word name (or the one-word name preceded by a title), and then, it will insert the punctuation you had originally placed after the character name.

---

A.  Enable "Use wildcards"

B.  *Find what:* ([\?\!.,'—...])(" ^32)(said)(^32)¬
    ([A-Z]*[^32])([A-Z]*)([!][A-z])

    *Replace with:* \1\2\5\6\4\3\7

C.  Use Selective Transposition (Choose "Find Next" or "Replace" as required)

---

**Explanation:** The "Find what" field contains seven expressions. The first includes all the terminators you might find preceding the close quotation mark in dialogue preceding an attribution. The second expression is the **close quotation mark** followed by a **space**. The third expression is the word **said** in lowercase (you already fixed any incorrectly capitalized instances of "Said" with the first search in this chapter). The fourth expression represents a **space** (**^32**). The fifth expression is a word that begins with a capital letter followed by any number of characters until a space is reached. The sixth expression is a word that begins with a capital letter followed by any number of characters. The seventh expression is any character that is not a letter. The "Replace with" field re-orders these elements correctly, as indicated by the numbers preceded by backslashes.

## 19) Global "Said She" and "Said He" Transposition

**Comment:** You can easily perform a global replacement of "said he" and "said she" with the correct forms "she said" and "he said."

| |
|---|
| A.   Enable "Use wildcards" |
| B.   *Find what:* **([\?\!.,' — …])(" ^32)(said)(^32)¬** **([she]{2,3})([!][A-z])** |
|      *Replace with:* **\1\2\5\4\3\6** |
| C.   Use Global Transposition |

**Explanation:** The "Find what" field contains six expressions. The first includes all the terminators you might find preceding the close quotation mark in dialogue preceding an attribution. The second expression is the **close quotation mark** followed by a **space**. The third expression is the word **said** in lowercase. The fourth expression represents a **space** (**^32**). The fifth expression is a new one. The letters **s, h,** and **e** are presented with the number of occurrences option set to **2 or 3,** meaning 2 or 3 of those letters. Of course, this will also try the words "se," "sh," "seh," "hse," and similar permutations of these three letters. The sixth expression is any character that is not a letter, and this is what filters out the cases "said her" which are dealt with in the next search. The reason for using wildcards is to permit a global transposition of both forms with a single click of the mouse button.

You might have broken this search into two non-wildcard searches (with "Match case" enabled) for **quote+said+space+he** and **quote+said+space+she,** replacing them with the correct forms. Unfortunately, this search would have also incorrectly picked up cases of "said her," and we want to save those for the next search. Moreover, it would have required two searches instead of one, and that would have taken more time in the 12-hour period we have allocated to complete the final edit.

## 20) Selective "Said" With Articles and Possessives Repair

**Comment:** Earlier in this chapter, we examined situations in which articles or possessives following "said" might justify a momentary suspension of the rules. Because each case requires a decision regarding whether the case qualifies as an exception to the rule, you will need to search for such patterns as a simple "Find" operation. Fortunately, we only need a single search pattern to reveal all or nearly all occurrences that might justify an exception.

---

A. Enable "Use wildcards"

B. *Find what:* ([\?\!.,'—...])("^32)(said)(^32)¬
([astheir]{1,5})(^32)

*Replace with:* \1\2\3\4\5\6 [does not change the found text]

C. This is a simple Find operation ("Find Next" or "Replace" will have the same affect)

---

**Explanation:** The "Find what" field contains six expressions. The first includes all the terminators you might find preceding the close quotation mark in dialogue preceding an attribution. The second expression is the **close quotation mark** followed by a **space (^32).** The third expression is the word **said** in lowercase. The fourth expression represents a **space (^32).** The fifth expression is a new one. The letters **astheir** are presented in brackets (meaning a subset of those letters can occur in any order) with the number of occurrences option set to the range 1 to 5 by the curly bracketed modifier. Permutations of subsets of these seven letters include "a," "the," "his," "her," "it," and "their," and this covers the vast majority of phrases you might have typed after "said" to refer the speaker. The sixth expression is **space** because another word will always follow the article or possessive pronoun that follows "said."

This search will also find "said she" and "said he" when those patterns are followed by a space, but this won't be a problem because you transposed all of those errors by performing the previous search; didn't you?

## Asked

"Asked" is the second-most common verb used in dialogue attributions.

Now that you have repaired all your attributions that use the word, "said," you should perform the same searches you performed for "said" replacing "said" with "asked." Following this paragraph, your will find the crucial transpositions (Searches #18a and #18b ) reproduced with "said" replaced by "asked" as models. Depending upon your personal writing style, you should decide whether you need to precede these with corresponding variations on Search #16 (capitalized forms), Search #17 (missing quotation mark), or both. Through awareness of your personal writing habits, you will also know whether you will need to follow these searches with corresponding variations on Search #19 (verb before subjective pronoun), Search #20 (verb before article or possessive pronoun).

The only thing altered in the searches below is that the target word "said" has been replaced by "asked" (in #21a and #21b). If you are aware of a specific attribution verb that you have used excessively, you may want to apply similar variations targeting that verb. For example, if one of your characters speaks using sign language, you might have more occurrences of the word "signed" than "asked." If you have used "thought" as a dialogue attribution verb, and have enclosed such thoughts with quotation marks, you may want to run the following searches (and possibly 16, 17, 19, and 20) with "thought" as the target.

## 21a) Global or Selective "Asked" with One-Word Character Name

**Comment:** This search is a variation on search 18a targeting "asked" instead of "said." See the comment for 18a for more information.

> A.  Enable "Use wildcards"
>
> B.  *Find what:* **([\?\!.,'—…])(" ^32)(asked)(^32)¬ (<[A-Z]\*[a-z]>)([!][A-z])**
>
>     *Replace with:* **\1\2\5\4\3\6**
>
> C.  Use Global or Selective Transposition (See the comment for 18a), but be careful if you go Global because of the asterisk. You may want to read the warning on page 46.

**Explanation:** See the explanation for search 18a; this is a variation of that search substituting "asked" for "said."

## 21b) Selective "Thought" with Two-Word Character Name

**Comment:** You can skip this if you have not used any of your characters' full two-word names in dialogue attributions, but don't skip it if you have used titles with a character's last name; for example, Dr. Smith, Mrs. Peacock, or Maj. Robertson. This search is a variation on Search #18b targeting "thought" instead of "said." See the comment under #18a for more information.

> A.  Enable "Use wildcards"
>
> B.  *Find what:* **([\?\!.,'—…])(" ^32)(thought)(^32)¬ ([A-Z]\*[^32])([A-Z]\*)([!][A-z])**
>
>     *Replace with:* **\1\2\5\6\4\3\7**
>
> C.  Use Selective Transposition (Choose "Find Next" or "Replace" as required)

**Explanation:** See the explanation for Search #18b; this is a variation of that search substituting "asked" for "said."

## Dialogue Proportions

In the beginning of this chapter we presented a list of alternate dialogue verbs with the admonishment that these be used for no more than 20% of your dialogue attributions, leaving 80% of your dialogue attributions to use "said" or "asked." You should have more than two times as many instances of "said" as you do of "asked" (2.33 times as many is a good ratio).

*insisted, shouted, answered, whispered, gasped, explained, demanded, cried, responded, lied, observed, murmured, stuttered, mumbled, snarled, screamed, protested, muttered, hissed, yelled, replied, groaned, begged, added, declared, confessed, railed, pleaded, conceded, whined, pointed out*

While searching for these and other dialogue verbs you may have employed incorrectly, it is a good practice to try to bring the additional verbs in line with those proportions. To do this, you must first calculate the total number of dialogue attributions in your manuscript, and then, subtract the number of those that used "said," "thought," or "asked." Fortunately, Word provides some tools to accomplish this, although those tools are not as precise as one might hope.

We can assume that nearly all occurrences of terminal punctuation followed by a close quotation mark represent an instance of dialogue. The attribution may come before the dialogue, after the dialogue, or in the midst of the dialogue. And there might be multiple sentences covered by a single dialogue attribution. "This is what I mean," he said, "by 'there might be multiple sentences covered by a single dialogue attribution.' Any number of sentences may come before the close quotation mark. This example has three." And, to complicate matters, there might be no dialogue attribution whatsoever, and the dialogue block might run across multiple paragraphs. In the latter case, the close quotation mark will not appear until the final paragraph, although each paragraph will commence with an open quotation mark.

To determine dialogue proportions as accurately as possible within the limitations of Word, we will first determine the total number of dialogue blocks, and then total the number of "said" and "asked" attribution verbs used. When we subtract that figure— the figure representing the number of normal attribution verbs— from the total number of dialogue blocks, we will be left with the number for exotic attribution verbs.

The number of common attribution verbs added to the number of exotic attribution verbs is your total number of attributions. As stressed throughout this chapter, the ratio between normal attribution verbs to exotic attribution verbs should be about four to one (80% to 20%).

Once we know our manuscript's ratio of normal to exotic dialogue attribution verbs, we will know whether to respond to the upcoming "Alternate Dialogue Verbs" searches by converting exotic verbs to "said" or "asked" or by reconfiguring passages of dialogue so attribution verbs are not required.

There is one missing part to this puzzle that will be revealed after you conduct the following dialogue proportion analysis.

## 22a) Dialogue Proportion Analysis (Step 1): Total Dialogue Blocks

**Comment:** Assuming that all dialogue blocks require terminal punctuation followed by a close quotation mark, the following search reveals the number of dialogue blocks within your manuscript, and, consequently, the maximum number of dialogue attributions.

---

A. Enable "Use wildcards" and switch from Replace mode to Find mode (use the tabs)

B. Enable "Highlight all items found in: Main Document"

C. *Find what:* ([\,\?\!\.\'])(\")

   *Replace with:* [empty] The "Replace with" field will not be visible in Find mode.

D. Press the "Find All" button and record the number of occurrences.

---

**Explanation:** The number revealed after you press the "Find All" button indicates the total number of dialogue blocks in your manuscript. Write this number down with the annotation, "total dialogue blocks."

## 22b) Dialogue Proportion Analysis (Step 2): Total with "Said"

**Comment:** When "said" is used as an attribution verb in direct dialogue, it is normally followed by a comma when it precedes the quoted dialogue, and by a period or a space when it follows the quoted dialogue. Unfortunately, a comma may also follow "said" for cases in which the dialogue continues because only the first phrase of the dialogue was stated before the attribution: "That possibility," he said, "confounds everything."

As if that were not enough, dialogue attributions may be embellished by present participles (these will be dealt with later in this chapter), otherwise we could simply search for **said+comma+space+open quotation mark**. For example: "That possibility," he said, wishing he were somewhere else, "confounds everything."

The situation is further confused because "said" followed by a space or even a comma occurs quite often in patterns of indirect dialogue—dialogue that does not require quotation marks.

Without lengthening the time required for this final edit, we cannot use Word's built-in tools to determine the number of occurrences of "said" in direct dialogue with complete accuracy. However, we can search for **said+comma** *plus* **said+period** *plus* **said+space** to glean an approximate number of direct dialogue attributions that include "said."

---

A. Enable "Use wildcards" and switch from Replace mode to Find mode (use the tabs)

B. Enable "Highlight all items found in: Main Document"

C. *Find what:* **(said)([,. ])**

   *Replace with:* [empty] The "Replace with" field will not be visible in Find mode.

D. Press the "Find All" button and record the number of occurrences.

---

**Explanation:** The "Find what" field contains the word **said** followed by a **comma, period,** or **space.** The three characters are enclosed in brackets indicating that any one will do. The number revealed after you press the "Find All" button indicates the approximate number of occurrences of "said" in your dialogue attributions.

As much as 25% or as little as 5% of your calculation may represent indirect dialogue. Because of this, multiplying your total by .75 to .95 will often produce a more accurate result. Only you can know how much indirect dialogue occurrences of "said" are normal for your work. Manually counting a small chunk—three representative chapters, for example—can make this number even more precise. Because Word will have highlighted all occurrences of **said+comma** and **said+period** and **said+space,** you might even consider scrolling through the entire document to make this final determination; the instances within indirect dialogue are easy to spot.

As inexact as this may be, it should be sufficient for our needs.

**Write down this number with the annotation,** *total said.*

## 22c) Dialogue Proportion Analysis (Step 3): Total with "Asked"

**Comment:** See the previous search. All the comments for "said" apply to "asked."

---

A.  Enable "Use wildcards" and switch from Replace mode to Find mode (use the tabs)

B.  Enable "Highlight all items found in: Main Document"

C.  *Find what:* **(asked)([,. ])**

   *Replace with:* [empty] The "Replace with" field will not be visible in Find mode.

D.  Press the "Find All" button and record the number of occurrences.

---

**Explanation:** The number revealed after you press the "Find All" button indicates the approximate number of occurrences of "asked" in your dialogue attributions.

"Asked" is used more than "said" in indirect dialogue because characters ask themselves things more often than they say things to themselves. As much as 30% or as little as 10% of your calculation may represent indirect dialogue. Because of this, multiplying your total by .70 to .90 will often produce a more accurate result. Only you can know how much indirect dialogue occurrences of "asked" are normal for your work. Manually counting a small chunk— three representative chapters, for example—can make this number even more precise. Because Word will have highlighted all occurrences of **asked +comma** and **asked+period** and **asked+space**, you might even consider scrolling through the entire document to make this final determination; the instances within indirect dialogue are easy to spot.

As inexact as this may be, it should be sufficient for our needs.

**Write down this number with the annotation, *total asked*.**

## How to Use Proportion Calculations

To use the numbers you gleaned from the previous four-step analysis, first add the "total said" number to the "total asked" number. Divide this number by the number of "total dialogue blocks." Multiply by 100.

**Write down result with the annotation, *% normal*.**

Here is the missing part of the puzzle. Attributions should be required in only 25% of your dialogue blocks. Note the term "dialogue blocks" in the previous sentence does not mean dialogue sentences. A dialogue block represents any number of dialogue sentences, as little as one, or as many as you like.

Professional writers manage to leave about 75% of all dialogue blocks without attributions because they take great care in structuring their dialogue so the reader always knows who is speaking. You can accomplish this by indicating the speaker in the first two dialogue paragraphs, and then letting the reader assume that the two speakers alternate until another attribution indicates otherwise or until non-dialogue text is encountered.

Another way to cue the reader about who is speaking is to use an action tag:

"I can't find any salsa." Laura had searched the refrigerator without success and now began to open the cabinet doors.

An action tag tells us who is speaking without using a speaking verb (attribution verb). Do not confuse action tags with the embellishment of an attribution verb by a present participle (verb ending in "ing"):

"I can't find any salsa." Laura said, opening the cabinet doors, one by one.

Moving on. We know that the best ratio between normal attribution verbs and exotic attribution verbs is 80% to 20%. So, if only around 25% of our dialogue blocks should have attributions, and 80% of those should be normal attributions, then 20% of your dialogue blocks should have the normal attribution verbs, "said" and "asked." The remaining approximately 5% of your attribution verbs can be drawn from the exotic pool.

**Examine the number you just wrote with the annotation % *normal*. It should be close to 20%. Is it?**

For example. You might have 3,000 dialogue blocks in you manuscript (noted as your "total dialogue blocks"). You should have around 600 normal attributions (the sum of your *total said* plus *total asked*). You will then be close to 20% for your % *normal* figure.

If your % *normal* figure is higher than 20%, your manuscript might be improved by cutting some normal attributions. If lower, you have some room to add, but you probably won't want to if you have crafted your dialogue to make it clear who is speaking.

Check the ratio between your "said" attribution verbs and your "asked" attribution verbs by dividing your *total said* by your *total asked*. Remember, you will usually have more than twice as many occurrences of "said" than "asked." A good figure to aim for is 2.33 (two and one-third) times as many occurrences of "said."

If you have far too many of one or the other and you discover that you are short on exotic attribution verbs, you may want to consider replacing some of your normal attribution verbs with those from the exotic collection.

In this example (3,000 dialogue blocks), because the ratio of your normal attribution verbs to your exotic attribution verbs should be about four to one, you should have about 150 exotic attributions, at most. 600 normal attributions plus 150 exotic attributions equals 750 total attributions interspersed throughout 3,000 dialogue blocks. 750 is exactly 25% of 3,000. Those 750 total dialogue attribution verbs break down into 600 normal plus 150 exotic, equivalent to an 80%–20% ratio. (These figures are approximate.)

## Alternate Dialogue Verbs

You should begin this section with the following information determined from the "How to Use these Calculations" section:

1) Whether or not you need to trim some normal attributions, and, if you're handy with math, you may have calculated approximately how many you need to add or trim.

2) Whether or not there is any leeway to convert a certain number of your normal attribution verbs to exotic forms.

3) Approximately how many attributions should contain verbs from the exotic lists (about 5% of the number you determined for your "total dialogue blocks" calculation).

4) Keeping the alphabetized list of acceptable exotic attribution verbs visible, you will be able to quickly see whether the alternate dialogue verbs uncovered by the next search need to be replaced.

5) You may also want to consult the list of acceptable exotic attribution verbs sorted by frequency in bestsellers visible, too, so that you can stay closer to proven norms.

6) Keep a piece of scratch paper handy. You will want to keep a tally of your exotic attribution verbs, if only by making a tick. If possible, make those ticks next to the corresponding verbs in the list ordered by frequency. You should have more of the verbs at the top of the list and progressively less and less as you near the middle, eventually the bottom group having only a single tick each.

Unfortunately, Word does not make it easy to target all dialogue attributions that do not use "said" or "asked," and don't forget that our earlier searches for those (#22b and #22c) were not 100% accurate. This notwithstanding, I have come up with a way to make stepping through all the dialogue go quickly enough to be valuable in the *Final Edit* process.

**The operation will involve three steps.**

1)  The attribution verbs from Searches #22b and #22c will be highlighted in a single step.

2a) We will step through the dialogue blocks using selective search, ignoring any results in the proximity of the highlighted normal attributions. Remember, we will be stepping through 3,000 dialogue blocks by pressing the Find Next button (or the Enter key). If you get a good rhythm going, you can step through 2 every second. At this speed, 3,000 dialogue blocks will take 25 minutes to step through. Remember that about 600 of these will be easy to spot as cases to ignore because the normal attributions, being highlighted, will jump off the page.

2b) While stepping through the dialogue blocks, quickly scan each case for exotic attribution verbs. Soon you will have the acceptable list memorized, if only in short-term memory. Make replacements as required, placing ticks next to the frequency list and keeping most of the ticks next to the top of the list.

2c) Pause periodically to calculate the total of your exotic verbs from the ticks. When it exceeds 5% of your total number of dialogue blocks, note where you are in your manuscript document. If you are halfway through and have already reached 5%, you will probably reach 10% by the end of the manuscript. You may want to backtrack and cut some exotic verbs. Alternatively, you may be satisfied with the fact that you will have at least replaced ridiculous verbs with those from the list that bestselling professional authors are using.

3) The attribution verbs that were highlighted in step 1 will have their highlights removed.

Steps 1 and 3 should take less than 5 minutes. Step 2 will take between 2 and 3 hours, depending upon the length of your manuscript. Figure you can edit from 30,000 to 40,000 words of your manuscript per hour while performing step 2.

Seasoned writers who have studied dialogue and observed the habits of the "masters" may be able to skip this process altogether. If so, proceed to the next section: "Additional Dialogue Details."

## 23a) Multi-Step Non-"Said" Dialogue Verb Replacements (Step 1)

**Comment:** This first step will highlight everything that was found in Searches #22b and #22c. Instead of performing this as 2 searches, a single, more complex search can be used to save time and steps. This one-stage search is not as accurate as performing highlighting variations of Searches #22b and #22c, but time is of the essence. If you feel this search highlights too many false positives, you can perform #22b and #22c again, this time replacing the found text with highlighted versions of the same. Before you take this step, you might want to use the following search string once with "Highlight all items found in: Main Document" enabled, and then compare the number of hits to the number you recorded with the annotation *% normal*. The difference between the two equals the number of false positives. There will not be many.

---

A. Enable "Use wildcards"

B. *Find what:* **(^32)(<[sa][as][ike]{1,2}d>)([,. ])**

   *Replace with:* **\1\2\3** (and choose a strong "Highlight" from the format menu while the cursor is in this field)

C. Replace All

---

**Explanation:** The "Find what" field contains three expressions. The first is a **space** (^32). The second looks for a word that begins with the letter "s" or "a" that is followed by the letter "s" or "a" (in the second position). These two letters will be followed by one or two of the characters "i," "k," or "e" and the resulting string of three or four letters will end with the letter "d." Very few words fulfill these requirements except for "said" and "asked." The third expression specifies that a **comma, period,** or **space** will follow the word constructed by the second expression.

Choose a strong highlight from the highlight colors available by way of either the toolbar or the formatting palette. All occurrences caught by the "Find what" wildcards will be highlighted with this color, because the "Replace with" specifies that each hit will be replaced by the three expressions in the "Find what" field in the same order: \1\2\3 and formatting will be applied.

## 23b) Multi-Step Non-"Said" Dialogue Verb Replacements (Step 2)

**Comment:** Assuming that all dialogue blocks require terminal punctuation followed by a close quotation mark, the following search will step through the close of every dialogue block in your manuscript. It is essentially the same as Search #22a, which was used to reveal the total number of dialogue blocks within your manuscript; however, this time, instead of counting the hits, the object is to quickly examine each dialogue block that does not contain a verb and that was highlighted in the previous step.

> A. Enable "Use wildcards" and switch from Replace mode to Find mode (use the tabs)
>
> B. *Find what:* ([\,\?\!\.\'])(\")
>
>    *Replace with:* [empty] The "Replace with" field will not be visible in Find mode.
>
> C. Selective Search: Either press "Enter" to proceed to the next hit, or close the Find box completely and step through your dialogue blocks using **Cmd+G** (Apple) or **Ctrl+Alt+Y** (Windows). Ignore the hit if it includes a highlight attribution verb, otherwise, examine it for possible revision.

**Actions:** As mentioned earlier in this section, while stepping through the dialogue blocks, quickly scan each case for exotic attribution verbs. Soon you will have the acceptable list memorized, if only in short-term memory. Make replacements as required, placing ticks next to the list of acceptable attribution verbs that is ordered by frequency while you try to keep most of the ticks next to the top of the list. If your total ticks exceed 5% of your total number of dialogue blocks, and you are halfway or less through your manuscript, you will probably reach 10% by the end. Consider backtracking to cut some exotic verbs…or not.

### 23c) Multi-Step Non-"Said" Dialogue Verb Replacements (Step 3)

**Comment:** This final step will remove the highlight from everything that was highlighted in step 1 of this multi-step search.

---

A.  Enable "Use wildcards"

B.  *Find what:* **(^32)(<[sa][as][ike]{1,2}d>)([,. ])**

   *Replace with:* **\1\2\3**   (and choose "Highlight" from the format menu after specifying "None" from the highlight colors available by way of either the toolbar or the formatting palette)

C.  Replace All

---

**Explanation:** See Search #23a for an explanation of this search. This search reverses the effect of that earlier search. Be sure to choose "None" as the highlight, either from the toolbar or the formatting palette, and then choose "Highlight" from the format menu while the cursor is in the "Replace with" field.

## Additional Dialogue Details

You can use Word's Find & Replace box to put the finishing touches on other aspects of dialogue. In this optional section, we will check multi-paragraph dialogue, paragraphs that open with a speaker attribution, correct usage of em dashes and ellipses in dialogue, dialogue adverbs, present participles in dialogue tags, and interior monologue.

### 24) Selective Multi-Paragraph Dialogue Check

**Comment:** Multi-paragraph dialogue spoken by the same character does not require a close quotation mark until the end of the final paragraph. To search for this, we will perform a selective search for **close quotation+return+open quotation mark** and replace the hits that reveal dialogue spoken by the same character with **return+open quotation mark** (dropping the close quotation mark from the previous paragraph). Some hits will be valid alternating dialogue paragraphs. Skip these unless you notice an extensive area of dialogue "ping-ponging" that might benefit from an action tag or even a speaker attribution. Use caution!

You may want to "Highlight all items found in Main document" before continuing. If the number is too high, it may merely indicate a good deal of alternating dialogue paragraphs, and if so, consider skipping this search.

---

A. Disable "Use wildcards" if it is enabled.

B. *Find what:* **"^p"**
[i.e., **close quotation+^p+open quotation mark**]

*Replace with:* **^p"** [**^p+open quotation mark**]

D. Selectively search, pressing the "Find" button or "Replace" button as required.

---

**Explanation:** The return character at the end of a paragraph is represented by the **caret+p (^p)**. For each hit that is a valid case of alternating dialogue, press the "Find" button to jump to the next hit without altering the previous one. For hits that reveal consecutive paragraphs of dialogue spoken by the same character, press the "Replace" button to strip the final quotation mark of the previous paragraph and jump to the next hit.

## 25) Selective Attributions Opening Paragraphs Revision

**Comment:** Except for extremely rare cases, including ones that call attention to themselves by inverting the normal order of speaker followed by attribution verb, paragraphs should never open with a dialogue attribution. Earlier searches should have repaired such cases that involve "said." Because 80% of your attributions should be "said" or "asked" this search is constructed to find paragraphs that commence with attributions using either of those verbs. By knowing your own writing style, you should be able to pinpoint similar errors involving exotic attribution verbs.

A.  Enable "Use wildcards" and switch from Replace mode to Find mode (use the tabs)

B.  *Find what:* **(^13)(*CharacterName*)(^32)¬ (<[sa][as][ike]{1,2}d>)(, "**

   *Replace with:* [empty] The "Replace with" field will not be visible in Find mode.

C.  Selectively search: Use **Cmd+G** (Apple) or **Ctrl+Alt+Y** (Windows) and revise as required.

D.  Repeat with each name on your character list.

**Explanation:** The "Find what" field contains five expressions. The first is the **return** character (**^13**) indicating the end of the previous paragraph. The second is the next name on your list of characters. The third is a **space**. The fourth is the familiar expression that resolves to "said" or "asked," and the fifth is a **comma+space+open quotation mark**.

**Variation:** After using this search with each of your character's names loaded into the expression in second position, you may want to also search for "He" and "She" in that position. Alternatively, you can substitute the following expression for those pronouns, which you will recognize as one that resolves to either "He" or "She" as required, and this will save you a step.

Substitute **([SHhe]{2,3})** for the character name so the "Find what" term becomes:

**(^13)([SHhe]{2,3})(^32)(<[sa][as][ike]{1,2}d>)(, "**

The second expression in the "Find what" files yields any 2-letter or 3-letter combination of the found characters **[SHhe]**. We need to provide the letter "H" in both capitalized and uncapitalized forms because the Find & Replace box is case sensitive when wildcards are enabled.

## 26) Selective Proper Use of Em Dashes & Ellipses in Dialogue Check

**Comment:** In dialogue, em dashes immediately before a close quotation mark indicate interruption, and ellipses in that position indicate a trailing off. This search will target either pattern and allow you to check whether or not you have used these symbols correctly.

In the case of an interruption indicated by an **em dash+close quotation mark**, the paragraph following the next paragraph will commence with an **open quotation mark** followed by an **em dash** if the interrupted character is allowed to finish his sentence by the interrupter. The opening **em dash** indicates the continuation of the interrupted dialogue. In this case, the interrupting paragraph should be between the interrupted paragraph and the continuation paragraph. For example:

"And I thought—"
"Are you doing my thinking again?"
"—That you might be interested."

Another type of interruption is possible. That is, when the interrupter finishes the sentence of the person he or she interrupted. For example:

"And I thought—"
"—That I might be interested. You can't be serious."

Sometimes, the interrupted sentence is never allowed to complete. In such cases, there will be no balancing **open quotation+em dash** for the interrupting **em dash+close quotation** that precedes it.

When it comes to em dashes, you should look for all three usages. Fortunately, ellipses are a much simpler matter, at least when used immediately prior to a close quotation mark. You only need to verify that they are used correctly, that is, to indicate a trailing off.

A. Enable "Use wildcards" and switch from Replace mode to Find mode (use the tabs)

B. *Find what:* **([ — ...])(" ^13)**

   *Replace with:* [empty] The "Replace with" field will not be visible in Find mode.

C. Selectively search: Use **Cmd+G** (Apple) or **Ctrl+Alt+Y** (Windows) and revise as required.

**Explanation:** The "Find what" field contains two expressions. The first resolves to either an **em dash** or an **ellipsis**. The second is a **close quotation mark** followed by a **return** indicated by **^13**. When wildcards are enabled, we must use **^13** to indicate the end of a paragraph instead of the **^p** symbol that we can employ when we are not using wildcards.

## 27) Selective Dialogue Attribution Adverbs Check

**Comment:** As you probably know, adverbs are words that used to "add" shades of meaning to verbs because we were too rushed or too lazy to stop and think of a better verb (one that would not require an adverb) when we first wrote the sentence. Most objectionable adverbs end in the suffix "ly," and these are all the more offensive when they modify a dialogue attribution verb. If you haven't exhausted your "quota" of exotic attribution verbs, you might exchanging attribution verbs for one that doesn't require an adverb. Alternatively, you may discover that the adverb that has managed to intrude within your dialogue attribution is actually modifying the subject of the dialogue rather than the dialogue verb. Such cases are much more obtrusive than adverbs that modify the attribution verbs.

**Compare:**

"Could he be the one?" she said, thoughtfully.
"Could he be the one?" she murmured.

**Compare:**

"Where have you been all my life?" he said, softly.
"Where have you been all my life?" he whispered.

In the second example, we are somewhat more tolerant of the "said softly" because "softly" actually modifies "said." Nonetheless, it is possible to write masterpieces without using a single adverb, and the fewer, the better.

Because attributions containing adverbs most often follow the adverb with a comma or a period, the search pattern will target those two configurations.

---

A. Enable "Use wildcards" and switch from Replace mode to Find mode (use the tabs)

B. *Find what:* **??ly[,.]**

   *Replace with:* [empty] The "Replace with" field will not be visible in Find mode.

C. Selectively search: Use **Cmd+G** (Apple) or **Ctrl+Alt+Y** (Windows) and revise as required.

---

**Explanation:** The "Find what" field contains two unspecified characters (**??**) because adverbs ending in *-ly* are always preceded by at least 2 characters. This is followed by the incriminating **ly** itself. Following this is the bracketed selection of a **coma** and a **period**, indicating that the search will find cases ending in either.

**Variation:** If you want to expand this search to include all adverbs in your manuscript, add a space inside the bracket set of possible adverb punctuators. Before you proceed, you should use "Highlight all items found in Main document" to count the number of cases you will be required to examine if you execute this variation. Make a note of this number because you may want to save this search for later, if any time remains.

The **[,.]** meaning **comma** or **period** will become **[,. ]** meaning **comma, period,** or **space.**

Search #47 expands this adverb search even more, but requires more time, as well.

## 28) Selective Dialogue with Present Participles Check

"Do I really have to learn this?" he asked, squirming in his chair.

**Comment:** In the previous sentence "squirming" is a present participle. Some authors feel that such embellishments actually enhance their dialogue attributions. In fact, present participles can add variety and motion to dialogue attributions *when used in moderation.* The following search will find present participles that follow either "said" or "asked." It should be performed six to eight times, or more, substituting the numbers 4 through 10, 11, 12, or more for the second number in the second set of curly brackets. This is due to a bug in Word that sometimes does not allow a second set of brackets to define a true range (more about this later).

---

A.  Enable "Use wildcards" and switch from Replace mode to Find mode (use the tabs)

B.  *Find what:* **(<[sa][as][ike]{1,2}d>)(, )(<[a-z]{1,4}ing)¬ ([!][a-z])**

   *Replace with:* [empty] The "Replace with" field will not be visible in Find mode.

C.  Selectively search: Use **Cmd+G** (Apple) or **Ctrl+Alt+Y** (Windows) and revise as required.

---

**Explanation:** The "Find what" field contains four expressions. The first expression resolves to either "said" or "asked." The second is a **comma** followed by a **space**. The third expression resolves to any word commencing with a lower case letter, and ending with the letters **ing** (all present participles end with "ing"). The second number in the second pair of curly brackets specifies exactly how many characters will precede the "ing" syllable. This is why you will need to perform the search multiple times.

 **(<[a-z]{3,3}ing)**  will find hoping but not wishing

 **(<[a-z]{3,4}ing)**  will find wishing, but not hoping or thinking

 **(<[a-z]{3,5}ing)**  will find thinking but not wondering

 **(<[a-z]{3,6}ing)**  will find wondering but not believing
 and so on…

**Explanation:** The model search above closes with a fourth expression, **([!][a-z])**, to ensure that the search finds words that end with "ing" alone, and not "ings" (such as "musings") or "ingly"

(such as "seemingly"). When you consider your personal style, you may want to drop that fourth expression and perform the search so that it allows all those other variations, many of which are troublesome.

## 29) Selective Interior Monologue Check

**Comment:** Interior monologue, also known as thoughts, never require quotes. Only spoken words require quotes. Because interior monologue is not spoken, it never requires an attribution.

To signal that we are hearing "inside" a characters head, interior monologue is presented in italics. The word "thought" is not required; in fact, in most cases it is redundant. Interior monologue often requires its own paragraph when a character doesn't speak, but thinks in response to another character's words. Italicized interior monologue may also alternate paragraphs when one is having an unspoken "dialogue" of thoughts with oneself.

The word "thought" may be used for non-italicized thoughts, the distinction is analogous to the difference between direct and indirect dialogue. Variants include *pondered, contemplated, reflected, speculated,* and *imagined.*

### Compare Thoughts vs. Interior Monologue:

Roger thought the cat's tail must have been clipped as he opened a can of tuna fish.

*That cat's tail has been clipped!* Roger opened a can of tuna fish in a vain attempt to absolve the human race for this atrocity.

### Compare: Indirect Dialogue vs. Direct Dialogue.

Her father had said she could go to the movies tonight if she wanted to.

Dad said, "You can go to the movies tonight, if you want to."

The selective interior monologue check is a simple search. We will examine all italicized passages and ensure that no unnecessary appearances of the word "thought" appear in their vicinity.

A. Disable "Use wildcards" and switch from Replace mode to Find mode (use the tabs)

B. *Find what:* [empty] but with the cursor in the field, choose Italics after selecting "Font" from the "Format" menu at the bottom of the Find & Replace box.

   *Replace with:* [empty] The "Replace with" field will not be visible in Find mode.

C. Selective search: Use **Cmd+G** (Apple) or **Ctrl+Alt+Y** (Windows) and revise as required.

**Explanation**: This search will step you through all italicized passages in your manuscript. Some hits will not be thoughts. Instead, they will be individual words and phrases that are italicized for emphasis or because they are foreign.

The ones in which we are interested will be longer, complete sentences or groups of sentences, even entire paragraphs. When you reach one of these, look around it for an un-italicized "thought" close to a character name or pronoun. In the vast majority of cases, these "thoughts" that form quasi-attributions are not required. You will probably be able to cut most of them, or transform them into action tags, removing the "thought" in the process.

# Chapter Seven

# Down for the Count

## Search for a Word; Replace it with Itself

You may have noticed that, starting in the previous chapter, counting the number of hits yielded by a search has started to become a determining factor in deciding what actions to take during a selective search or whether to run a particular search at all. In fact, pre-counting hits will become increasingly important as we move to more subjective types of editing—*content* editing. Until now, we have been concerned with corrections of *form*. There is no sense examining 100 occurrences of a certain phrase if 100 occurrences of that phrase are below the threshold at which the phrase becomes objectionable.

In coming searches, you will sometimes need to know what percent of a certain pattern is tolerable. Moreover, you will want to be able to convert that percentage into a number that relates to your document. If the evidence suggests that 50% of your paragraphs is a good number of paragraphs to begin with dialogue (those paragraphs will all begin with an open quotation mark), then you need to be able to convert that percentage 50% into a real number. If your manuscript has 4,400 paragraphs, then 50% of those represent 2,200 paragraphs.

You can count hits using the Find & Replace box in two ways. You can search for a word, phrase, or wildcard pattern and replace it with itself; the total number of occurrences displayed in the resulting dialog box will be the number of hits. Alternatively, you can load the "Find what" field, put the Find & Replace box in Find mode by hiding the "Replace with" field (use the tabs at the top of the Find & Replace box), and press the "Find All" button with the "Highlight all items found in Main Document" enabled. This latter approach will display the number of occurrences right in the Find & Replace box; it is often the fastest way to discover the count.

Previous searches requiring counts have drawn out the explanation process to great length. For example, Search #22a) to count the number of dialogue blocks:

> A. Enable "Use wildcards" and switch from Replace mode to Find mode (use the tabs)
>
> B. Enable "Highlight all items found in: Main Document"
>
> C. *Find what:* (\[\,\?\!\.\'\])(\")
>
> *Replace with:* [empty] The "Replace with" field will not be visible in Find mode.
>
> D. Press the "Find All" button and record the number of occurrences.

In the future, counts such as this will be represented with the following abbreviated format in which the first column is the search string when wildcards are enabled and the second column is the version you can use if you prefer not to enable wildcards. For many of the searches in this book, wildcards are required so this will indicate "[none]" as is the case below.

| Wildcard Search String | No Wildcards | Comments |
|---|---|---|
| (\[\,\?\!\.\'\])(\") | [none] | Total number of dialogue blocks. |
| (^32)(<[sa][as][ike]{1,2}d>)([,. ]) | [none] | The number of "said" or "asked" dialogue attributions |

| Use this information: | |
| --- | --- |
| Divide ("said" or "asked" attributions) by (total dialogue blocks) | |
| Multiply the result by 100. | This is the percent of your dialogue blocks that contain "said" or "asked" attribution verbs. |
| Research suggests this number should be close to 20%. | |
| Divide ("said" or "asked" attributions) by 5 | |
| Research suggests this number should be the approximate number of "exotic" attribution verbs used in your manuscript. | |

Keep a pen and paper handy. You will want to take notes, keep running totals, and perform calculations such as the ones above.

## Chapter Eight

# Search & Rapid Rewrite

## Tips for the searches on the following pages:

In this chapter you will learn how to target specific known-to-be-troublesome areas for rapid rewrite, including the beginnings of paragraphs and sentences, passive voice problems, and extraneous past perfect verbs.

To search for words at the beginning of paragraphs use ^p followed by the word (without quotes and without spaces) while wildcards are disabled.

Searching for problem words at the beginnings of sentences would seem to be as simple as searching for a capitalized form of a word that would not appear capitalized for any other reason than being the first word in a sentence, such as searching for all capitalized instances of "There" or "It" with *case sensitivity* enabled. However, some words we would like to target will be capitalized no matter where they occur within a sentence—character names, for example.

After we search for paragraph starters and chapter openers, we will examine the ends of these larger building blocks in our manuscript. Then we will search through the innards. But before we commence, we should have a clear idea of what we are trying to accomplish with our rewriting.

Great paragraphs are often reducible to self-contained stories in themselves. The same concept can apply to individual sentences. And a significant number of paragraphs consist of only one sentence. Consider the following paragraph from the novel *Winter Moon* by Dean Koontz, a 50-word single-sentence paragraph that is practically a story in itself:

> Although he appeared to be rough enough to walk into a biker bar and take on a mob of machine wranglers, the attorney was soft-spoken and so polite that Jack was aware of how badly his own manners had deteriorated under the constant abrasion of daily life in the city.

Observe how Dean Koontz provides enough background about the attorney that we start to think the sentence is about him, until suddenly we are firmly in Jack's point of view, moving toward Jack's reaction. This is like a camera pulling back for a wider shot.

Koontz often opens important statements with a tip disclosing how we should interpret what is about to be said: "Although he appeared" serves that function in this case. Moreover, "Although" cues us of a coming inevitable concession or contrast; "he" makes us wonder to whom the pronoun refers; and "appear" injects a things-are-not-as-they-appear tension.

Next, "rough enough to walk into a biker bar" is already an evocative image, which, at first glance, needs no further clarification, yet "and take on a mob of machine wranglers" ramps up the image another forty-five degrees on the psychological dial.

The comma closes the first of four chunks of information.

Now, the master author answers some of the questions we have been wondering about: "the attorney" answers our questions about the initial pronoun, while "soft-spoken and so polite" provides the promised inevitable contrast inherent to the resolution of the things-are-not-as-they-appear problem. That is the end of the second chunk and the end of the first half of this little story.

Suddenly, we must execute a 180-degree turn regarding who we thought the sentence is about: it's not even about the attorney; it's really a sentence about "Jack," and not simply about his presence, but about the things he "was aware of." We must reinterpret the former material from Jack's POV, and realize that merely the attorney's surprising appearance (he was not what he appeared to be) was enough to make Jack "aware of how badly his own manners had deteriorated." This certainly reveals a great deal about the gulf between the attorney's soft-spoken politeness and the current deteriorated state of Jack's manners, while it also makes us ask ourselves the question: "What caused Jack's manners to deteriorate?" at the end of chunk three. This might provoke us to ask whether our own manners are similarly deteriorating or at risk.

Koontz then answers this question: "the constant abrasion of daily life in the city" caused his manners to deteriorate.

Masterfully, through this very clarification, Koontz causes us to ask another question with this final chunk: obviously if Jack's manners had deteriorated, they must have started out in a less-deteriorated state. This, coupled with the phrase "abrasion of daily life in the city" implies that at one time, Jack probably lived in a place quite different from the city—a place from which one might visit the city, but certainly not on a "daily" basis, and certainly not enough for one's life to undergo "constant abrasion" from the experience.

"What is Jack's background?" we wonder.

In the symmetrically placed beginning chunk, we were given a certain amount of background about the other actor (the attorney), so that we now want an equivalent depth of information about Jack. As long as the author can get us to keep asking questions, we will keep reading onward to discover the answers, even if it means staying up long past our bedtimes.

Always pay special attention to the last word or phrase of Koontz's interesting sentences and strategically-placed paragraphs, and particularly, to single-sentence paragraphs; they almost always point forward, another way to compel us to keep turning the pages. The last phrase in this single-sentence paragraph is "life in the city." The miniature story, a veritable slice of life, could aptly be titled, "Life in the City,"

This one sentence paragraph uses a technique sometimes called that I call progressive disclosure. New information requires us to rethink or re-interpret what we have learned previously. The author forces us to ask questions and then chooses which ones he will answer immediately and which he will leave for later in the story, suspended in time for the moment (unresolved), making us read on and on and on, searching for the answers.

I hope that this brief lapse into subjective analysis will give you some ideas as you head into the rewriting section of *Final Edit*.

## Initial Words in Paragraphs and Sentences

The following searches deal with the initial words in paragraphs and sentences. Later in this section, the searches will address the first words of chapters as well as chunks that are smaller than a chapter but usually larger than a paragraph. When performing the searches in this group, keep in mind that two consecutive paragraphs or sentences that begin with the same word can be jarring. More than two, unless used for special effect, is practically unheard of. This is one time the often-stated "rule of three" does not apply.

> Do any sentences begin with the words ``There" or ``It"? They can almost certainly benefit from revision. (Compare: There were three gunmen who had sworn to kill him. It was hard to believe. or: Three gunmen had sworn to kill him. He couldn't believe it.)                  —Crawford Kilian

### 30a) Targeting Paragraph Starters is/was/were/seemed (There and It)

**Comment:** The first rewrite search will target paragraphs that begin with "There is," "There was," "There were," "There seemed," "It is," "It was," and "It seemed." You should not use many of these. Bestselling professional authors might start some paragraphs with "There was" and "It was," but rarely any of the other patterns that this search will find. "There was" is used as a paragraph starter less than 1% of the time. "It was" is used even less than that. Although these two ("There was" and "It was") are seen as paragraph starters in small numbers (less than 1%), they are hardly ever seen as the start of the first paragraph in a chapter (Charles Dickens once famously got away with "It was" as an opening line).

> A. Enable "Use wildcards" and switch from Replace mode to Find mode (use the tabs)
>
> B. *Find what:* **(^13)([TherIt]{2,5})(^32)([wearsi]{2,4})**
>
> *Replace with:* [empty] The "Replace with" field will not be visible in Find mode.
>
> D. Selectively search: Use **Cmd+G** (Apple) or **Ctrl+Alt+Y** (Windows) and revise as required.

**Recommendation:** Before or after dealing with all these "There is/was/were/seemed" and "It is/was/seemed" paragraphs, you may want to take a count of your total number of paragraphs so you can monitor the frequency of these undesirable paragraph starters.

| Wildcard Search String | No Wildcards | Comments |
|---|---|---|
| (^13)([A-Z"]) | [none] | Total number of paragraphs |
| (^13)(There was) | ^pThere was<br>^pThere is<br>^pThere were | Paragraphs beginning with "There" followed by "was," "is," or "were" |
| (^13)(It was) | ^pIt was<br>^pIt is | Paragraphs beginning with "It" followed by "was" or "is" |

Your total number of paragraphs will also include chapter headings and the like. Subtract the number of paragraphs found in each chapter heading before proceeding. Other special features such as embedded songs or poems may skew this number. Subtract the number of returns in these elements as well.

The following "Use this information" table explains more about what you should do with the data you obtain doing these counts.

| Use this information: | |
| --- | --- |
| Divide (Number of paragraphs beginning with "There was") by (total paragraphs) | |
| Multiply the result by 100. | This is the percent that start with "There was" |
| Research suggests this number should be close to 20%. | |
| Divide (Number of paragraphs beginning with "It was") by (total paragraphs) | |
| Multiply the result by 100. | This is the percent that start with "It was" |
| Research suggests this number should be well under 1%. | |

## 30b) Targeting Paragraph Starters is/was/were/seemed (He and She)

**Comment:** Paragraphs that begin with "He is," "He was, "He seemed," "She is," "She was," and "She seemed," are also objectionable and can usually be improved by replacing the offensive usage with an action verb.

> A.  Enable "Use wildcards" and switch from Replace mode to Find mode (use the tabs)
>
> B.  *Find what:* **(^13)([SHhe]{2,3})(^32)([wasei]{2,3})**
>
> *Replace with:* [empty] The "Replace with" field will not be visible in Find mode.
>
> D.  Selectively search: Use **Cmd+G** (Apple) or **Ctrl+Alt+Y** (Windows) and revise as required.

**Explanation:** The second expression in the "Find what" field has been changed to resolve to "He" or "She." The final expression in the "Find what" field has been changed from **([wears]{3,3})** to **([wasei]{2,3})** because neither "He" nor "She" can logically take the verb "were" at the beginning of a sentence.

False positives are possible with this search.

## 30c) Targeting Paragraph Starters is/was/were/seemed (Characters)

**Comment:** Paragraphs that begin with one or more of your characters' names followed by "was," "were," or "seemed" can often be improved by substituting an action verb in place of the offending usage. This search targets such patterns but may produce some false hits as did the previous search (Ignore these). You will need to repeat this search for each of your characters. Insert the character's name in the "Find what" string in place of *CharacterName* in the example below.

> A. Enable "Use wildcards" and switch from Replace mode to Find mode (use the tabs)
>
> B. *Find what:* **(^13)(*CharacterName*)(^32)([wearsi]{2,4})**
>
> *Replace with:* [empty] The "Replace with" field will not be visible in Find mode.
>
> D. Selectively search: Use **Cmd+G** (Apple) or **Ctrl+Alt+Y** (Windows) and revise as required.

**Explanation:** The final expression in the "Find what" field has been changed from **([wase]{3,3})** to **([wears]{2,4})** because it is possible that your subject might be plural and be followed by a "were." For example: *Jack and Jill were starting to walk up the hill.*

## 31a) Targeting Sentence Starters is/was/were/seemed (There and It)

**Comment:** Sentences that begin with "There is," "There was," "There were," "There seemed," "It is," "It was," and "It seemed," even when not at the beginning of a paragraph, may be objectionable. Substituting a **space (^32)** for the **return (^13)** in the previous search will target all remaining sentences beginning with these words. Sentences at the beginnings of paragraphs will be ignored; presumably, you checked these using the previous searches.

> A. Enable "Use wildcards" and switch from Replace mode to Find mode (use the tabs)
>
> B. *Find what:* **(^32)([TI][herIt]{1,4})(^32)([wearsi]{2,4})**
>
>    *Replace with:* [empty] The "Replace with" field will not be visible in Find mode.
>
> D. Selectively search: Use **Cmd+G** (Apple) or **Ctrl+Alt+Y** (Windows) and revise as required.

**Explanation:** The second expression in the "Find what" field has been changed to resolve to "There" or "It" (capitalized).

**Recommendation:** Before or after dealing with all these "There is/was/were/seemed" and "It is/was/seemed" paragraphs, you may want to make a count of your total number of paragraphs so you can monitor the frequency of these undesirable paragraph starters.

## 31b) Targeting Sentence Starters is/was/were/seemed (He and She)

**Comment:** Sentences that begin with "He was, "He seemed," "She was," and "She seemed," are also objectionable and can usually be improved by replacing the offensive usage with an action verb. This search targets those patterns but will also produce false positives; for example, "He saw" and "She saw." You should ignore such false hits.

> A. Enable "Use wildcards" and switch from Replace mode to Find mode (use the tabs)
>
> B. *Find what:* **(^32)([SHhe]{2,3})(^32)([wasei]{2,3})**
>
>    *Replace with:* [empty] The "Replace with" field will not be visible in Find mode.
>
> D. Selectively search: Use **Cmd+G** (Apple) or **Ctrl+Alt+Y** (Windows) and revise as required.

**Explanation:** The final expression in the "Find what" field has been changed from **([wears]{3,6})** to **([wasei]{2,3})** because neither "He" or "She" can logically take the verb "were" at the beginning of a sentence.

## 31c) Targeting Sentence Starters it/was/were/seemed (Characters)

**Comment:** Sentences that begin with one or more of your characters' names followed by "is," "was," "were," or "seemed" can often be improved by substituting an action verb in place of the offending usage. This search targets those patterns but may produce some false hits as did the previous search. You will need to repeat this search for each of your characters. Insert the character's name in the "Find what" string in place of *CharacterName* in the example below.

---

A.  Enable "Use wildcards" and switch from Replace mode to Find mode (use the tabs)

B.  *Find what:* **(^13)(*CharacterName*)(^32)([wearsi]{2,4})**

   *Replace with:* [empty] The "Replace with" field will not be visible in Find mode.

D.  Selectively search: Use **Cmd+G** (Apple) or **Ctrl+Alt+Y** (Windows) and revise as required.

---

**Explanation:** The final expression in the "Find what" field has been changed from **([wase]{3,3})** to **([wearsi]{3,4})** because it is possible that your subject might consist of more than one character's name and therefore be followed by a "were."

32) Targeting Paragraph and Sentence Starters with variations of Search #30 and #31

**Comment:** So far, the searches in this chapter have been concerned with locating objectionable sentence starters in which a pronoun or character name is followed by "was," "were," and "seemed." However, other verbs besides those three, if overused, may also become objectionable and are subject to improvement by the substitution of an action verb.

Examples include: *appeared, began,* and *started.*

Your genre or personal writing style may result ing your having added the word "to" to these: *appeared to, began to,* and *started to.*

If you have time and your propensity for error is high, you may wish to include the following forms as well: *had seemed to, had appeared to, had begun to, was beginning to, had started to,* and *was starting to.*

## Sample Variations on Search #30 (a, b, and c) and #31 (a, b, and c)

| Source Search | Find what (was/were/seemed) | Substitutions |
|---|---|---|
| Paragraph starters (There, It) | (^13)([TherIt]{2,5})(^32)¬ *(Substitution)* | appeared<br>began<br>started |
| Paragraph starters (He, She) | (^13)([SHhe]{2,3})(^32) ¬ *(Substitution)* | |
| Paragraph starters (Characters) | (^13)(*CharacterName*)(^32)¬ *(Substitution)* | appeared to<br>began to |
| Sentence starters (There, It) | (^32)([TI][herIt]{1,4})(^32)¬ *(Substitution)* | started to<br>had seemed to |
| Sentence starters (He, She) | (^13)([SH][he]{1,2})¬ (^32)(*Substitution*) | had appeared to<br>had begun to |
| Sentence starters (Characters) | (^13)(*CharacterName*)(^32)¬ *(Substitution)* | was beginning to<br>had started to<br>was starting to |

To search for words at the beginning of sentences without using "case sensitive" because the particular word is always capitalized (character names, city names, etc.), use the tip above ^p and four additional searches:

> period+space+theWord
> questionMark+space+theWord
> exclamationMark+space+theWord
> closeQuote+space+theWord.

## 33a) Targeting Other Objectionable Paragraph Starters (pronouns)

**Comment:** Besides the classic cases that were addressed in Searches #30, #31, and #32, paragraphs that begin with any pronouns or verbs can usually be improved. Pronouns require antecedents (the noun they stand for), and, except in highly controlled circumstances, they require their antecedent to come before their own initial mention; in fact, as close as possible—there may be no intervening nouns—to their first occurrence. In the previous sentence, "Pronouns" is the antecedent of the pronouns "they" and "their" that follow it.

If the writing is extremely clear, an antecedent appearing in the final sentence of a previous paragraph is often strong enough to carry forth to the next paragraph again, as long as there are no intervening nouns (including proper nouns such as character names). But this is rarely the case with the first paragraph of a chapter or the first paragraph following a double line-break implying a passage of time, change of point of view, new location, or any combination thereof, known as a hiatus (sometimes referred to by a poetry term: *caesura*). Some such pauses contain a blank line with three or four asterisks (**return+return+\*\*\*+return+return**), the asterisk placeholder often being replaced by a dingbat at the book design stage, although such indications are usually reserved for breaks that are higher in the structural hierarchy.

If you are running late, you may want to examine only the first paragraphs of chapters and chunks of text following a hiatus. The variations following this set, will address those.

---

A. Enable "Use wildcards" and switch from Replace mode to Find mode (use the tabs)

B. *Find what:* **(^13)([IYHSWT][tyouhey]{1,3}^32)**

   *Replace with:* [empty] The "Replace with" field will not be visible in Find mode.

D. Selectively search: Use **Cmd+G** (Apple) or **Ctrl+Alt+Y** (Windows) and revise as required.

---

**False Positives:** This search will find paragraphs that begin with the word "The" along with all the pronouns (except "I").

**Closer Reading Required:** While examining the beginnings of your paragraphs, keep an eye out for the following constructions. Often you can delete everything up to and including the "that" in order to tighten the flow.

- *It is (or was, has, has been, etc.) [noun phrase or verb phrase]* **that**
- *You are (or were, have, have been, had., had been, etc.) [noun phrase or verb phrase]* **that**

- *He is (or was, has, has been, etc.) [noun phrase or verb phrase]* **that**
- *She is (or was, has, has been, etc.) [noun phrase or verb phrase]* **that**
- *We are (or were, have, have been, had., had been, etc.) [noun phrase or verb phrase]* **that**
- *They are (or were, have, have been, had., had been, etc.) [noun phrase or verb phrase]* **that**

## 33b) Targeting Other Objectionable Paragraph Starters (possessives)

**Comment:** Possessive pronouns also require antecedents (the noun they stand for). Acceptable usage adheres to the same considerations as nominative pronouns; however, possessives are treated with a good deal more tolerance, particularly if their antecedent follows very soon after—usually within a window that opens at the last noun or pronoun of the previous paragraph and closes no later than the first word of the second sentence of the paragraph in which they occur.

Again, if you are running late, you may want to examine only the first paragraphs of chapters and text following a hiatus, and the variations following this set deal with those particular cases.

---

A. Enable "Use wildcards" and switch from Replace mode to Find mode (use the tabs)

B. *Find what:* **(^13)([YHIO][oietu][usr]{1,2})(^32)**

   *Replace with:* [empty] The "Replace with" field will not be visible in Find mode.

D. Selectively search: Use **Cmd+G** (Apple) or **Ctrl+Alt+Y** (Windows) and revise as required.

---

**Variations:** This search will not find "My," "Your," or "Their." Substitute **(^13)([MY][your]{1,3})** for the first two expressions of this search to target "My" and "Your." Substitute **(^13)(Their)** for the same two expressions to target "Their."

## 33c) Targeting Other Objectionable Paragraph Starters (conjunctions)

**Comment:** Coordinating conjunctions overused as the first words of paragraphs are confusing to many readers. "And" and "But" are tolerated more than the others, light usage of which can be acceptable when the pacing is fast. The following search targets all the FANBOYS (*For And Nor But Or Yet So*) when they appear as the first word of a paragraph, except those that are only two letters in length ("Or" and "So").

As with all the searches of group #33, if you are up against a deadline, you may want to examine only the first paragraphs of chapters and those following a hiatus. The variations following this set will address those.

---

A. Enable "Use wildcards" and switch from Replace mode to Find mode (use the tabs)

B. *Find what:* **(^13)([FANBY][onuretd]{2,2}^32)**

   *Replace with:* [empty] The "Replace with" field will not be visible in Find mode.

D. Selectively search: Use **Cmd+G** (Apple) or **Ctrl+Alt+Y** (Windows) and revise as required.

---

**False Positives:** This search will find paragraphs that begin with the word "Not," "Are," "You," and several other less common 3-letter words.

**Variations:** This search will not find "Or" or "So." Substitute **(^13)([OS][ro])(^32)** for the "Find what" string to target "My" and "Your."

## 33d) Targeting Other Objectionable Paragraph Starters (misc.)

**Comment:** The following list is long. It contains more than 140 words or phrases designed to cover a variety of genres. As with all long lists in this book, you should cross out the items you never use as the first word of a paragraph to make this list as short as possible. You may disagree with some of the terms on this list because you have verifiable knowledge that specific terms are common in the genre of your writing. Cross those out too.

While you examine the ones that are usually objectionable, you may find opportunities to insert first words that actually help the reader comprehend what is about to be stated. You can use the first word or phrase to lead the reader by telling him or her how to interpret an entire passage. You can create bias in the reader, and though this is akin to "leading the witness" in a court of law, it is nonetheless a good practice in writing. Many of these phrases are simply adverbs or adverbial phrases, but depending upon whom you are talking to, such words are called "mood changers" or "leading phrases."

Such phrases help orient readers at the beginning of sentences to any change of mood, time, or location from the previous sentence. A few examples: *But, Yet, However, Nevertheless, Still, Instead, Therefore, and Thus;* including those that cue a state of mind: *Neither agitated nor lethargic, With less than a full smile, Rolling his eyes, On a hunch,* as well as those that cue a period of time: *Meanwhile, Now, Later, Today, By late afternoon, Subsequently, This time, Suddenly, Before leaving, Previously, When, On the evening of, A few minutes later, Just before dark, Two days later, For the third time, At some point, Eventually;* and those that cue a change of location: *Elsewhere, Behind the building, On the left, and In the master bedroom.* Mood changers can also help the reader form an interpretation of what is about to come: *Ironically, Oddly, Like a mirage, So much for the, The worst had happened; It couldn't get worse; After a hesitation, Instead of, Indeed, Inevitably, On reconsideration, To make matters worse, Evidently,* and so forth.

In *On Writing Well,* (amzn.to/OnWritingWell) William Zinsser considers *But* to be the strongest of these, because it lets the reader know that what is coming in the paragraph that follows will be in total contrast to what has preceded it. Substitute *However* if you find your manuscript contains too many *Buts.* The temporal mood changers can also save the reader much confusion (*Meanwhile, Now, Later,* etc.).

If time is becoming an issue, you may want to examine only the first paragraphs of chapters and those following a hiatus. The variations following this set will address such cases.

A. Enable "Use wildcards" and switch from Replace mode to Find mode (use the tabs)

B. *Find what:* **(^13)(*term from "Mood Changers" list*)(^32)**

*Replace with:* [empty] The "Replace with" field will not be visible in Find mode.

D. Selectively search: Use **Cmd+G** (Apple) or **Ctrl+Alt+Y** (Windows) and revise as required.

The list of Mood Changers is on the next page.

## Mood Changers

| | | |
|---|---|---|
| Above all | In the background | Really |
| Accordingly | In the coming days | Seemingly |
| Add to this | In the distance | Similarly |
| After all | In the final analysis | Simultaneously |
| A key feature | In the first place | Sooner |
| All in All | In the forefront | Specifically |
| Also | In the foreground | Straight ahead |
| Alternatively | In the meantime | Strategically |
| Analogous to | In the same way | Such as |
| Apparently | In the second place | Surrounding |
| By that time | In truth | Then again |
| By the same token | Indeed | This being |
| Certainly | It follows that | Till |
| Concurrently | It is apparent | To be sure |
| Consequently | Lest | To begin with |
| Contrarily | Likewise | To conclude |
| Conversely | Mainly | To continue |
| Due to | More importantly | To enumerate |
| During the | Moreover | To explain |
| Equally important | Most important | To illustrate |
| Even more | Namely | To list |
| Even so | Naturally | To reiterate |
| Even though | Nearby | To repeat |
| Firstly | Nearer | To sum up |
| Formerly | Nevertheless | To summarize |
| Further | No matter | To this end |
| Furthermore | Noteworthy | Too |
| Generally | Notwithstanding | Truly |
| Granted that | Occasionally | Unabashedly |
| Hence | On one hand | Unbelievably |
| Here again | On the contrary | Under those circumstances |
| However | On the side | Undoubtedly |
| In addition | On the whole | Unexpectedly |
| In any event | On top | Unfortunately |
| In brief | Only if | Unless |
| In case | Only when | Unthinkably |
| In conclusion | Opposite | Unthinkingly |
| In contrast | Ordinarily | Whenever |
| In detail | Otherwise | Wherever |
| In like fashion | Out of sight | While it may be true |
| In like manner | Periodically | While it my not be true |
| In order to | Predictably | While this may be true |
| In particular | Presumably | While this may not be true |
| In short | Previously | With the result that |
| In similar fashion | Primarily | With this in mind |
| In similar manner | Provided | With this purpose in mind |
| In spite of | Provided that | Within sight |
| In summary | Rather | |

## 34) Targeting Chapter Openings with Variations of Search #33

**Comment:** The comments for the previous set of searches (Search Series #33) admonished you to skip ahead to Searches #34 and #35 if you were running out of time. A simple substitution will help you target only chapter openings. Be sure to read the comment for the following search (Search #35) before deciding which to do first, or whether to do this search (Search #34) at all.

The previous searches identified paragraphs by placing a return (^13) before any of the search expressions. The following list contains the most common methods used to search for chapters. These examples provide the expression or expressions you should place in front of any of the #33 Search Series you choose to apply at the chapter level exclusively. The search strings (contents of the "Find what" field) described in the following will replace the initial (^13) expression in each of the series #33 searches.

**1) "Chapter" or numbers (or both) in your chapter titles:** If the word "Chapter" is in your Chapter title, and the word is followed by a one or two digit number, you can precede the main expressions in the #33 Search Series with:

**(Chapter)(^32)([0-9]{1,2})(^13^13).**

This will pick up cases of the word "Chapter" followed by a space (^32), followed by a 1-digit or 2-digit number, which is followed by two returns (^13^13). If you have faithfully performed the basic searches in this book, you will have no more than two returns anywhere in your manuscript.

If your manuscript extends to 3-digit chapter numbers, change the "number of occurrences" part of the chapter number expression to {1,3} resulting in the following variation:

**(Chapter)(^32)([0-9]{1,3})(^13^13)**

**2) Your chapter titles consist of numbers only:** If the word "Chapter" does not occur in your chapter titles, then delete the first two expressions of the previous example. Substitute the following:

**([0-9]{1,2})(^13^13)**

If your manuscript extends to 3-digit chapter numbers, change the "number of occurrences" part of the chapter number expression to {1,3} resulting in the following variation:

**([0-9]{1,3})(^13^13)**

**3) Your chapter headings share the same Word style:** Word allows you to assign styles to various classes of elements in any document. Typical styles include "Heading 1," "Heading 2," "Heading 3," and more, but in a book, you will eventually want to have a *Title* style and possibly a *Subtitle* style for your title page, and maybe an *Author* style for that page, too. You may want specific styles for your *Frontal-Matter Headings*, or simply use your *Chapter Title* style. Some manuscripts will require a *Chapter Subtitle* style and one or more levels of *Headings* and *Sub-heading* styles. Most of your text will use a *Body Text* style, and you may require a *Block Quotation* style. If your work has figures, you may need a *Caption* style.

One advantage of styles is that you can change the look of an element once (for example, the size and font of your chapter titles) and this will change all the other chapter titles in your book, provided they have been assigned the *Chapter Title* style. Styles will save your book designer and eBook conversion service many hours and possibly, many days. This should save you many dollars.

The style that pertains to this particular search is the *Chapter Title* style or the style used for that purpose. It will be necessary to delete any words in the "Find what" field and search only on the basis of formatting style. With the cursor in the "Find what" field, use the "Formatting" popup menu at the bottom of the Find & Replace box and choose the style of your chapter titles (or subtitles) after selecting "Style" from that menu. It's best to disable the "Use wildcards" option in this scenario.

**4) None of the above apply:** In spite of this, at least you have differentiated your chapter titles by using either a different typeface (e.g. Arial or Helvetica), a different font style (e.g. bold), a different font size, or a different alignment (e.g., centered) or a combination of any or all of those characteristics. Don't worry. There's a search for that.

As in the previous example, it will be necessary to delete any target text and search only for the formatting using the "Formatting" popup menu at the bottom of the Find & Replace box. Choose the specific characteristics shared by all your chapter titles (or subtitles) after selecting "Font" or "Paragraph" from that menu. It's best to disable the "Use wildcards" option in this scenario.

**Special note for variations of pronoun searches:** The first paragraphs in chapters do not have the luxury of a previous paragraph in which to disclose a pronoun's antecedent, so such antecedents usually appear no later than the first word of the second sentence of the paragraph in which the pronoun occurs.

**Action:** Armed with one of the four search variations just stated, return to Search Series #33 and perform the substitute searches accordingly.

### 35) Targeting Openings Following a Hiatus: Variations of search #33

**Comment:** The comments for the previous set of searches (Search Series #33) admonished you to skip ahead to Searches #34 and #35 if you were running out of time. A simple substitution will help you target chapter openings only.

The previous searches identified paragraphs by placing a **return** (^13) before any of the search expressions. You can include the first paragraphs after a hiatus by simply changing that single return to a double **return** (^13^13). This will also target the first paragraphs in chapters., so you may want to perform this search instead of the previous one.

If you want to target only those paragraphs that follow a hiatus containing a dingbat, add whatever character string you have used to indicate dingbats, for example: (\*\*\*^13^13). In the previous example, because three asterisks were used to indicate this type of hiatus and the asterisk has a special meaning with wildcards enabled, it was necessary to use the escape backslash before each one. Alternatively, you could have disabled "Use wildcards" and used the simple form: ***^p^p, but this would mean giving up the true search targets, the pronouns, the "to be" verbs, and so forth. It is not an expeditious tradeoff.

**Special note for variations of pronoun searches:** The first paragraphs in chapters or chunks following a hiatus do not have the luxury of a previous paragraph in which to disclose a pronoun's antecedent, so the antecedents usually appear no later than the first word of the second sentence of the paragraph in which the pronoun occurs.

**Action:** Armed with one of the two search variations just stated, return to Search Series #33 and perform the substitute searches accordingly.

## The "Power Position"

The beginnings of paragraphs, sections, and chapters were the subject of the last group of searches. You probably know that the first paragraphs of chapters are extremely important. A similar honor is afforded the first sentence of paragraphs, and, as we demonstrated with the last group of searches, the first word of sentences. These elements propel us into the chapter, sentence, or paragraph. But another location may even be more important—the ends of these elements. With this in mind, we will turn to the ends of paragraphs, sections and chapters—the areas that are often referred to as the "power position," and this has nothing to do with Feng Shui.

The last paragraph of chapters or sections, the last sentence of paragraphs, and the last word of sentences are the elements that keep us moving forward. When it comes to the ends of chapters and sections, the final paragraph or sentence, sometimes even the last word, is what makes us turn the page. These are the silver bullets of page-turners.

> "The last word is the one that lingers in the reader's ear." — William Zinsser, *On Writing Well*

We located the beginnings of chapters by searching for two returns in a row: **^13^13** (with wildcards enabled) or **^p^p** (without wildcards enabled). The final searches of the previous batch (#34 and #35) provided some alternative methods for targeting these locations. We will use similar patterns to locate these closing power position elements.

## Maximizing the power position effect

You may be asking, *What do I do once I've located the ends of my chapters?* The answer is, you will rewrite the last word, sentence, or paragraph to maximize the power position effect. Here is an example to clarify this:

**Example**: The last paragraph in Chapter 2 of *The Testament* by John Grisham:

> "Stop!" someone yells, and they're moving behind me. No one has seen me walk in a year. I grab the handle and open the door. The air is bitterly cold. I step barefoot onto the narrow terrace which borders my top floor. Without looking below, I lunge over the railing.

The wheelchair-bound character that we presume to be the protagonist has been presented (in first person) as completely rational, albeit somewhat calculating, throughout the first two chapters of the novel, a chunk that is nearly 4,000 words long. We are as surprised as the other characters by the event in this last paragraph. It ends with a *That changes everything* sentence—one that forces us to turn the page with such rapidity that it is as if the very paper were burning our fingertips. At this moment, we know with absolute certainty that this book will be a page-turner.

The first five sentences of the paragraph in question don't give a clue about what is coming. The protagonist could simply be longing for a breath of fresh air and we have no reason to suspect what is about to happen. However, when read in retrospect, those five sentences set up the suicide perfectly. They could precede the taking of a breath of fresh air, or they could precede a suicide. Because suicide has not been hinted at, the notion doesn't cross the reader's mind. The opening of the paragraph could and did function as a fork in the road. It was, in fact, the proverbial double-edged sword, and we have just received an unanticipated blow from the edge of least expectation.

The impact of this event is strengthened by the power position effect. Imagine if the paragraph had ended with the sentence "I lunge over the railing without looking below." Your high school English teacher probably told you, with good reason, never to end a sentence with a preposition. By this point in your career, you may have forgotten that "rule," you may be rebelling against such "rules" (in the name of *originality*), or you may have seen so many violations of the rule in well known books, even bestsellers, that you assume that the world of writing has evolved to embrace the "do your own thing" philosophy that now shapes the rest of the world.

Wrong! As a consummate author, Grisham knows that one word (*railing*) changes everything that has gone before and sets up everything that is to come. He is well aware that for maximum effect, the word should be placed in the power position of the sentence, of the paragraph, and ultimately, of the chapter. Even the words "lunge over" do not tip-off the outcome. The character is very old; old people fall very often; "lunge over" could mean the character has simply fallen to the floor, perhaps due to the shock of the "bitterly cold" air.

The word "railing" is what discloses the real intention of the character. It is the game-changer. The moment we read that word, we begin asking questions (provoking questions in the reader is a good thing, by the way): *Aren't they on the 14th floor? Why would he do such a thing? How could he commit suicide being as sane as he is? Did I miss some fatal flaw by reading too quickly? How does this change everything that has transpired up until this point? Will it be necessary to re-interpret any or all previous events because of this tragedy? What could possibly happen next now that the main character is dead? Or did he survive the fall?* We are still reeling from the event long after the character has hit the pavement.

When you find your own chapter-ending sentences that resemble "I lunge over the railing without looking below," change them to "Without looking below, I lunge over the railing." This is why we target the final paragraphs of each chapter. Of course, many paragraphs might be improved by this technique, but at this point in the *Final Edit* process the deadline may loom too close to check all of them. If you do have the time, you will recall that the endings of all paragraphs become targets if the search term is simply ^p (without wildcards) or ^13 (with wildcards).

## 36) Targeting Chapter Endings for Power Position Effect

**Comment:** Use whichever of the following search strings is most appropriate for your manuscript or with which you are most comfortable. At least three popular ways to end chapters: 1) with a manual page break (^m); 2) with a section break (^b or ^12); or 3) with two returns ^p^p or ^13^13) followed by the word Chapter+space+a number. Use whichever conforms to your writing style. Keep in mind that there is no wildcard search available for a manual page break.

> A. Disable "Use wildcards" and switch from Replace mode to Find mode (use the tabs)
>
> B. *Find what:* ^m or ^b or ^p^pChapter ^? or ^p^m
>
>   *Replace with:* [empty] The "Replace with" field will not be visible in Find mode.
>
> C. Selectively search: Use **Cmd+G** (Apple) or **Ctrl+Alt+Y** (Windows) and revise as required.

**Explanation:** In the third example search string, a ^? appears as the last element because your chapters may be titled "Chapter 1" or "Chapter One," that is, with a number or a letter. You may want to replace that with either ^# (to indicate numbers only) or #$ (to indicate alphabetic characters only). If you use the second search string but instead of closing your chapters with two returns you close with a single return followed by a manual page break, you should substitute ^p^m for that search; you will not need to add the word "Chapter" and following as in the example. Note that in the example search above, there is a **space** after the word **Chapter**

in non-wildcard mode, and that could be a **^32** if you are using wildcards.

**Variation:** The same search with wildcards enabled:

> A. Enable "Use wildcards" and switch from Replace mode to Find mode (use the tabs)
>
> B. *Find what:* **^12 or ^13^13Chapter^32[A-Z0-9]**
>
> *Replace with:* [empty] The "Replace with" field will not be visible in Find mode.
>
> C. Selectively search: Use **Cmd+G** (Apple) or **Ctrl+Alt+Y** (Windows) and revise as required.

## 37) Targeting Section (Chunk) Endings

**Comment:** You can target the last paragraphs before a hiatus by using as your search string a double return (**^p^p** or **^13^13**). This will also target the last paragraphs in chapters if you have ended chapters with two returns.

If you want to target only those paragraphs that precede a hiatus containing a dingbat, add whatever character string you have used to indicate dingbats, for example: **^p^p\*\*\*** or **^13^13\\*\\*\\***). In this example, because three asterisks were used to indicate this type of hiatus and the asterisk has a special meaning with wildcards enabled, it is necessary to use the escape backslash before each one. If you use another character for dingbats, for example, a symbol, be sure to substitute that for the three asterisks.

> A. Disable "Use wildcards" and switch from Replace mode to Find mode (use the tabs)
>
> B. *Find what:* **^p^p or ^p^p\*\*\* or ^p^m**
>
> *Replace with:* [empty] The "Replace with" field will not be visible in Find mode.
>
> C. Selectively search: Use **Cmd+G** (Apple) or **Ctrl+Alt+Y** (Windows) and revise as required.

**Explanation:** The first option in the "Find what" field targets all hiatuses, the second will target only the ones before dingbats, and the third will target chapter endings that include a manual page break.

**Variation:** The same search with wildcards enabled offers a another option in the "Find what" field.

A. Enable "Use wildcards" and switch from Replace mode to Find mode (use the tabs)

B. *Find what:* **^13^13** or **^13^13[!\*]** or **^13^13\\*\\*\\***

   *Replace with:* [empty] The "Replace with" field will not be visible in Find mode.

C. Selectively search: Use **Cmd+G** (Apple) or **Ctrl+Alt+Y** (Windows) and revise as required.

**Explanation:** The first option in the "Find what" field targets all hiatuses, the second will target all hiatuses except the ones before dingbats, and the third will target only the ones before dingbats.

**Variation:** If your chapters close with a single return, and you want your search to include all chapter breaks within your hiatus search, you should do the previous "no wildcards" search.

## Showing vs. Telling

You have heard the maxim: *show, don't tell.* Writing teachers and pundits refer to this distinction by labeling some passages "scenes" and others, "summaries" or "sequels." Politicians and lawyers have a saying for the same problem when it occurs in their speeches and other orations: "If you're explaining, you're losing." I prefer to think of the distinction between "showing" and "telling" as relating to events presented in real time versus those presented in non–real time.

Is it possible to target instances of "telling" as in "showing vs. telling" using Word's Find & Replace box?

No, not all of them. But we can target quite a few by searching for verbs of awareness; *saw, watched, heard, felt, tasted, smelled, thought, pondered, noticed, realized, knew, seemed, seeming, appeared, appearing, looked, looking,* and *sounded* are some of the most common. These verbs usually signal that we are about to read a report about something happening rather than a blow-by-blow, action-packed dramatic event happening in real time (You can recognize many instances of telling by the fact that they do not occur in real time). If you or one of your characters uses any of these verbs, a good deal of telling is about to ensue, all or most of which can be rewritten so that it shows the same information instead of telling the reader about it.

When a character recounts something instead of living it before our very eyes (the eyes of our imagination), both the character and the action move farther away from the realm of our imagination. Immediacy dissipates. Instead of being immersed in the plot, we are suddenly removed to a point from which we are only hearing about it, or reading about it as the case may be. Suddenly, we become aware of the fictive dream receding in the distance, if only because we have just stepped out of it, or, more accurately, been pushed out of it by an author who is letting a character explain to us what is happening, rather than letting us experience it ourselves. Some people visualize this process as the author having placed the character *between* the reader and the action.

Granted, searching for verbs of awareness is not going to highlight up all of your transgressions of telling, but it will reveal enough of these abominations to make a difference; that is, if you rewrite those passages.

### Transforming Telling into Showing

When asked about how to convert telling passages to showing passages, editors often proclaim: *Involve the senses! Don't simply act, feel!* Involving the senses, the feelings, whether physical (sight, hearing, taste, smell, touch) or emotional (feeling a need, a longing, an absence or presence) in real-time, without an "interpreter" between the reader and the action recounting the events, is one way to craft a sentence, paragraph, or scene so that it shows us what is happening.

Rewriting a *telling* passage can involve many small steps. If you consider such activity to be a hassle, you should examine the sketchbooks of Beethoven (amzn.to/BeethovenSketches). Even with four symphonies already to his credit, his step-by-step reworking of the themes and melodies in the *Fifth Symphony* is revealed as a protracted labor of love, one that resulted in creating a work that many consider to be immortal.

As architect Louis I Kahn so succinctly stated, "The creation of art is not the fulfillment of a need but the creation of a need. The world never needed Beethoven's Fifth Symphony until he created it. Now we could not live without it." If you imagine that such great works in any art form come in a single inspiration, without requiring the extensive polishing of one's craft, or perhaps they come in a dream that merely awaits its being written down, then you are the one who is dreaming.

As Thomas Edison said in 1903, "Genius is 1 percent inspiration and 99 percent perspiration." In other words, it's about craft, no matter what the field of endeavor.

## *Example*

The following example is from Koontz's *The Taking*. This is the first paragraph of chapter 8:

> "Until now, Molly had never felt a need to take a loaded pistol to the bathroom."

Now consider the editing progression that might have lead to the construction of this information-packed one-liner. I have no idea whether Dean Koontz actually followed these steps, but I have seen developmental progressions like the following hypothetical one used by other authors.

> Molly took a pistol into the bathroom.
>
> [This is what actually happened. This is telling.]

Molly took a loaded pistol into the bathroom.

> [If the gun is loaded it might go off. This adds excitement.]

Molly had never taken a loaded pistol to the bathroom before.

> [This puts the sentence in the negative (associated with bad outcomes) and declares this is a first time occurrence (anything could happen).]

Molly had never taken a loaded pistol to the bathroom until now.

> [The word "now" instead of "before" creates immediacy. The event is brought closer. Increased relevance!]

Until now, Molly had never taken a loaded pistol to the bathroom.

> [By inverting the order, to lead with immediacy, the uncommon location is placed in the power-position.]

Until now, Molly had never felt a need to take a loaded pistol to the bathroom.

> [Adding "felt a need" recasts the sentence to express a feeling rather than an objective statement. This is the published version of the sentence.]

When you rewrite passages during your final edit, you might not break down your the transformation into discrete steps; it is possible that the perfect rewrite will come to you as a single thought. But if it doesn't, I remind you to remember Beethoven's sketches. They provide ample testimony to the effectiveness of such step-by-step processes.

## Caveat

Some of the hits resulting from the following searches may turn out to be valid usages, deep in the throws of real-time drama. These do not need to be altered. Knowledge of your personal writing style may prompt you to add the qualifiers *to, like, as if,* or *though* (and occasionally *that*) to the core verbs of awareness on the following list.

## Verbs of Awareness

see, saw, saw that
watch, watched
heard, heard that
feel, felt, felt like, felt as if, felt as though
feels like, feels as if, feels as though
taste, tasted, tasted like, tasted as if, tasted as tough
tastes, tastes like, tastes as if, tastes as though
smell, smelled, smelled like, smelled as if, smelled as though
smells, smells like, smells as if, smells as though
thought, thought that
ponder, pondered, ponder whether
notice, noticed, noticed that
realize, realized, realized that
knew, knew that
seem, seemed, seemed to, seemed like, seemed as though
seems, seems to, seems like, seems as though
seeming, seeming to, seeming like, seeming as if, seeming though
appear, appears, appeared to, appeared as if, appeared as though
appearing, appearing to, appearing like, appearing as if, appearing though
look, looked like, looked as if, looked as though
looks, looks like, looks as if, looks as though
looking like, looking as if, looking as though
sound, sounded like, sounded as if, sounded as though
sounds, sounds like, sounds as if, sounds as though

## 38) Targeting Verbs of Awareness

**Comment:** The list is above. You may want to search for only the first words of each group or you may know that it would be more effective for you to search for some of the variations. As with other lists in this book, feel free to cross out the terms you know that you never use so that you do not waste precious time searching for them.

A. Disable "Use wildcards" and switch from Replace mode to Find mode (use the tabs)

B. *Find what:* [terms from the list of verbs of awareness]

   *Replace with:* [empty] The "Replace with" field will not be visible in Find mode.

C. Selectively search: Use **Cmd+G** (Apple) or **Ctrl+Alt+Y** (Windows) and revise as required.

## 39a) Targeting Verbs of Initiation

**Comment:** Just as things that only *seem* to be happening or *appear* to be happening create distance between the reader and the action, so do things that *begin* to happen or *start* to happen, and their variations: *began* to happen, *started* to happen, or are *beginning* to happen or *starting* to happen. Moreover, sentences using such patterns tend to be in telling passages as opposed to showing passages, although valid uses exist for the latter. *Commence, commenced,* and *commencing* should also be on this list if you are known to use it. Ditto for *stood* and *turned.* As with other lists in this book, feel free to cross out the terms you know that you never use so that you do not waste time searching for them.

### Verbs of Initiation

| |
|---|
| begin, began, beginning to<br>start, started, starting to<br>commence, commenced, commencing<br>stood to, stood and<br>turned to, turned and |

| |
|---|
| A. Disable "Use wildcards" and switch from Replace mode to Find mode (use the tabs)<br><br>B. *Find what:* [terms from the list of verbs of initiation: forms of begin, start, and commence [see the comment]<br><br>*Replace with:* [empty] The "Replace with" field will not be visible in Find mode.<br><br>C. Selectively search: Use **Cmd+G** (Apple) or **Ctrl+Alt+Y** (Windows) and revise as required. |

## 39b) Targeting Specific Distancing Constructions

**Comment:** Three constructions add excess distance between the reader and the text being read, if only by causing a bump in the road of comprehension, one that might require a reread: *had had, is is,* and *that that.* Recognizing that something is amiss, but not being able to pinpoint the problem, some writers will insert a comma between the repeated words in an effort to repair what they sense is an error: *had, had*; *is, is*; and *that, that*. Usually, that is not the optimal solution. These patterns can show up anywhere, although they seem to be more prevalent in passages that are telling rather than showing.

Important: Surround *is is* with spaces when you search for it (**space+is+space+is+space**) to eliminate false positives. Also, *is, is* (with a comma between the otherwise adjacent words) occurs much more often now that the English language is deteriorating. Therefore, you should always include the comma-separated forms in your searches.

A. Disable "Use wildcards" and switch from Replace mode to Find mode (use the tabs)

B. *Find what:* [terms from the repeated constructions mentioned in the comment]

*Replace with:* [empty] The "Replace with" field will not be visible in Find mode.

C. Selectively search: Use **Cmd+G** (Apple) or **Ctrl+Alt+Y** (Windows) and revise as required.

# Chapter Nine

# Substitution Searches

Nadia Boulanger, world-renowned music teacher of the 20th century, once said of the Beethoven *Archduke Trio,* "change one note from one of the chords and everything is spoiled." She said something similar about Stravinsky's *Symphony of Psalms* it all depended on "one note in the oboe." Misplace one note and it's ruined.

You may not think so, but misusing one word in your manuscript can ruin it. According to Noah Lukeman in *The First Five Pages* (amzn.to/TheFirstFivePages), if the mistake happens in, you guessed it, the first five pages, your manuscript is likely to end up in the rejection pile. The reason is slightly different than the Boulanger–Beethoven example; Lukeman's point is that errors occurring on the first five pages will likely occur with the same frequency throughout the rest of the book.

Don't forget the children who might read text containing your error, or the impressionable young at heart. How do you think we ended up with the majority of the population saying things like "Myself and my wife were walking on Main Street when it happened"?

As you look through the following lists, pick out additional problem words that only you can know are in your manuscript, because you will remember typing them.

Targeting word after word in the various substitution searches forces you to skim your text repeatedly, a process that will pick up speed with every successive search. I have found that conducting such searches, with all the necessary focusing on individual words in paragraphs, puts me in a "zone" in which it is easier to notice words that appear multiple times in the same sentence. Although using a word twice or thrice in a single sentence is not always a bad thing particularly for rhythmic reasons or parallelisms, when a word appears two or more times in the same sentence with two or more *meanings*, the reader becomes confused.

Pronouns have a habit of causing this error, and the word "that" often creates similar problems. In a sentence, this befuddlement can never be tolerated.

> "Surprisingly often a difficult problem in a sentence can be solved by simply getting rid of it."
> —William K. Zinsser

In a paragraph, the reader will tolerate multiple meanings of "that" as long as they appear in different sentences and far enough apart. Pronouns enjoy a similar freedom in paragraphs. However, if the recurring word or phrase is one that stands out or otherwise calls attention to itself (e.g., "penguin"), the reader will be less forgiving.

Repeated words, when each instance has a different meaning, is one of many problems that cannot be targeted using the search patterns and tools we have studied in this book. For this reason, keeping one's eye alert to that error while the other eye checks the context of your search hits is all the more important.

Again, in *The First Five Pages* (amzn.to/TheFirstFivePages), Noah Lukeman advises, "Cut. Most sound problems, including repetition, echoes, alliteration, rhymes, and poor sentence fragments, can be fixed by simple cutting."

## The Worst of the Worst

This part of *Final Edit* includes many lists of words to avoid— words to target either for replacement or deletion: lists of "flab" words, vague words, boring words, plague words, and redundancies. If you flip ahead through this chapter, you may become nervous. You have done a few searches involving lists of words in the previous chapter and you know how tedious the process can become. Your time may be running out. You may have to pick and choose among the lists to still have time for the wildcard searches interspersed among them.

Some of these avoidable words are found on several different lists of problem words and phrases; a handful appear on multiple lists in this chapter (those are accompanied by an asterisk to let you know that you have already searched for them if you have performed all the searches up to that point, although they will not have an asterisk if the earlier search was case sensitive); others occur only once within this book but are found on many lists that did not make it into this book. There are almost sixty words or phrases in this "multi-listing" category.

The nearly 60 words that form this list may be considered the worst of the worst. For purposes of a final edit against a deadline, you may feel it more expedient to search for the words in this list and skip the rest of the lists in this chapter. This approach will give you more time for the remaining wildcard searches.

The worst of the worst is presented as two lists. The first list (#40a) consists of 45 words; it assumes that you did the "Showing and Telling" searches in the previous chapter and omits the verbs of awareness. The second list (#40b) is adds the 12 worst of the verbs of awareness and the 2 worst of the verbs of initiation in case you skipped the "Showing and Telling" searches. Taken together, the two lists are the "Hall of Shame" for this chapter. If you have time for only one more repetitive substitution list search, make sure it is this one, otherwise, skip this and proceed to "Cut the Flab Words." But if you do skip this search in favor of performing the rest of the searches in this chapter, remember that the words appearing with an asterisk are found on multiple lists and consequently appear on the "Worst of the Worst" list. Let those asterisks alert you to the most undesirable items on the lists.

These are simple searches with wildcards disabled and no case sensitivity. Most of the rest of the substitution list searches will take the same format as the first one.

## 40a) Optional "Worst of the Worst" Words and Phrases

**Comment:** Read the introduction preceding this search for more details. As with other lists in this book, feel free to cross out the terms you know that you never use so that you do not waste time searching for them.

---

A. Disable "Use wildcards" and switch from Replace mode to Find mode (use the tabs)

B. *Find what:* [terms from the list of "Worst of the Worst" (Words and Phrases)]

   *Replace with:* [empty] The "Replace with" field will not be visible in Find mode.

C. Selectively search: Use **Cmd+G** (Apple) or **Ctrl+Alt+Y** (Windows) and revise as required.

---

### The Worst of the Worst (Words and Phrases)

| | | |
|---|---|---|
| accordingly | had had | rather |
| almost | however | really |
| apparently | in order to | some |
| as of | indeed | somewhat |
| as to | ironically | suddenly |
| certainly | it was | that |
| could | just | that that |
| down | just then | the fact that |
| due to | knew | there was |
| eventually | lots of | too |
| felt | most | truly |
| get | now | unfortunately |
| got | predictably | up |
| firstly | previously | very |
| | | would |

## 40b) Optional "Worst of the Worst" Verbs of Awareness & Initiation

**Comment:** See the introduction preceding the search for detailed more details. As with other lists in this book, feel free to cross out the terms you know that you never use so that you do not waste time searching for them.

> A. Disable "Use wildcards" and switch from Replace mode to Find mode (use the tabs)
>
> B. *Find what:* [terms from the list of "Worst for the Worst" (Verbs of Awareness & Initiation)]
>
> *Replace with:* [empty] The "Replace with" field will not be visible in Find mode.
>
> C. Selectively search: Use **Cmd+G** (Apple) or **Ctrl+Alt+Y** (Windows) and revise as required.

### Worst of the Worst (Verbs of Awareness & Initiation)

| | | |
|---|---|---|
| appeared | realized | seems to |
| appears | saw | started |
| began | seemed | tasted |
| heard | seemingly | thought |
| looked | seems | |

# Cut the Flab

The master teachers, writers, and editors William Zinsser and Sol Stein identify certain words and phrases as detrimental to prose. Sol Stein refers to these as "flab" in his valuable reference *Stein on Writing* (amzn.to/SteinOnWriting): "Flab, if not removed, can have a deleterious effect on the impatient reader, who will pay less attention to each word and begin to skip. In *On Writing Well* (amzn.to/OnWritingWell), William Zinsser mentions this in the "Bits and Pieces" chapter. This search brings together problem words noted by both these authorities.

## 41) Trim Flab Phrases

**Comment:** As with other lists in this book, feel free to cross out the terms you know that you never use so that you do not waste time searching for them.

> A. Disable "Use wildcards" and switch from Replace mode to Find mode (use the tabs)
>
> B. *Find what:* [terms from the list of "Flab Phrases" list]
>
>    *Replace with:* [empty] The "Replace with" field will not be visible in Find mode.
>
> C. Selectively search: Use **Cmd+G** (Apple) or **Ctrl+Alt+Y** (Windows) and revise as required.

### Flab Phrases

| | | |
|---|---|---|
| a bit | equally as well | lots of |
| a little | far from | on a daily basis |
| a pair of | had had | on the order of |
| all too | had ought | on the basis of |
| almost like | hadn't ought | one of the most |
| as to whether | having said that | pretty (as in pretty bad) |
| at such time as | in a number of | prior to |
| being as | in a very real sense | seem to |
| being that | in most cases | seems to * |
| by means of | in order to | should of |
| by a factor of | in order that | so as to |
| close to | in regards to | some kind of |
| could of | in some cases | somewhat like |
| due to | in terms of | sort of |
| due to the fact that | in the event that | suppose to |
| the fact that | is found to be | that said |
| each and every | just then | that that |
| | | would of |

# Vanquish the Vague, Annihilate Ambiguity

Words that are vague or ambiguous disorient the reader. Such words can interrupt the rhythm, pace, and flow of a story because they cause the reader to stop and attempt to determine exactly what you had in mind. When the reader is forced to stop in this manner, he or she is no longer absorbed in your story. The reader awakens from the fictive dream intent on analyzing the puzzle your vague or ambiguous word presents and does not read a word further, until the problem is solved. The tension or suspense subsides; the drive toward the resolution or climax loses energy; the connection or identification with a favorite character fades. For some readers, this jarring disruption might consume only a fraction of a second, for others, seconds or minutes. When presented with too many attention diverting gaps of this kind, most readers will do the one thing you are trying to prevent at all costs: they will put down the book. You should consider such prose as the direct opposite to the kind that is found in a page-turner.

## 42a) Vanquish Vague Words

**Comment:** As with other lists in this book, feel free to cross out the terms you know that you never use so that you do not waste time searching for them. The words with an asterisk have appeared on at least one other list in the book so far. Consequently, if you have performed all the searches up until this point, you can skip those. If you haven't, consider those to be slightly more objectionable than the others.

> A. Disable "Use wildcards" and switch from Replace mode to Find mode (use the tabs)
>
> B. *Find what:* [terms from the list of "Vague Words"]
>
>    *Replace with:* [empty] The "Replace with" field will not be visible in Find mode.
>
> C. Selectively search: Use **Cmd+G** (Apple) or **Ctrl+Alt+Y** (Windows) and revise as required.

The list of Vague Words appears on the following page.

## Vague Words

| | | |
|---|---|---|
| a bit * | fairly | respective |
| a little * | finally | seemingly |
| about | here | simply |
| actually | highly | slightly |
| almost | just | so |
| almost like * | kind of | some |
| already | knew * | somehow |
| always | most | somewhat |
| appears * | mostly | somewhat like * |
| approximately | nearly | sort of * |
| basically | now | successive |
| close to * | perhaps | then |
| could | practically | there |
| down | pretty * | truly |
| entire | quite | up |
| even | rather | utterly |
| exactly | really | very |
| | | would |

**Comment:** Bestselling author Jerry Jenkins has stated that it may be possible to get rid of all occurrences of "up."

## 42b) Conquer Ambiguous Contractions

When the reader cannot determine the meaning of a word by the way it is spelled, then the word is ambiguous. Ambiguity is a type of vagueness that can work to the advantage or disadvantage of your book. Controlled ambiguity is the double-edged tool with which misdirection, red herrings, and surprise endings are fashioned. In the final edit, we are concerned with the other kind: unintentional ambiguity.

Many words have the potential to introduce ambiguity. Of these, a collection of contractions is among the most abused: ambiguous contractions. Maybe this is because people use contractions in speech during which the listener uses other cues—facial expressions and tone of voice—to deduce meaning. Your reader does not have the luxury of these non-verbal clues.

**Comment:** While you read the following rules, remember that the damage of ambiguous contractions does *not* extend to dialogue. When it comes to dialogue, anything goes. You are presenting an aspect of a character's individuality with dialogue.

You certainly can't help it if that character speaks with ambiguous contractions!

1) Do not use personal pronouns with contractions **apostrophe+d,** because these can mean either *had* or *would*.

*I'd, you'd, he'd, she'd, it'd, we'd they'd, who'd*

2) A similar problem can occur with the contraction **apostrophe+s** because it can mean *is* or *has* (never *was*).

*he's, she's, it's, that's, there's, what's, who's*

3) Many **-'ve** contractions should be written out.

*could've, would've, should've, must've, might've and that've*
*could have, would have, should have,*
*must have, might have, that have*

4) Also write out *I'd've* as either *I'd have* or *I would have*. The same goes for those involving *you, he, she, it, they,* and *we*.

5) Write out *there're* as *there are* because it can sound like *they're*, which is another contraction you should write out for the same reason.

6) With the exception of **apostrophe+t** (*wasn't, hadn't, shouldn't*) you should write out contractions if using them does not reduce the number of syllables in the resulting contracted word. The first three in the following list are already discouraged because they are ambiguous (*had* or *would*), so now you have another reason to write them out.

*this'd, that'd, and what'd, this'll, that'll, when'll, where'll, that're, when're*

## Wildcard searches

| Contracted Words | Contraction | Find what: |
|---|---|---|
| I, you, he, she, it, we, they, who | 'd | ([^32^13\"])¬ ([IiYyHhSsWwTteouy]{1,4}'d) |
| he, she, it, that, there, what, who | 's | ([^32^13\"])¬ ([HhSsIiTtWwweaor]{2,5}'s) |
| could, would, should, must, might, that | 've | ([^32^13\"])¬ ([CcWwSsMmTtouldsigha]{4,6}'ve) |
| I, you he, she, it, we, they | 'd've | ([^32^13\"])¬ ([IiYyHhSsWwTteouy]{1,4}'d) |
| they, there | 're | ([^32^13\"])([Ttheyre]{4,5}'re) |
| this, that, what, when, where | 'd, 'll, 're | ([^32^13\"])¬ (^32)([TtWwhiaestnr]{4,5}'[dlre]{1,2}) |

**Comment:** The first expression in the "Find what" field allows the contraction to appear as the first word of a paragraph or internal sentence, inside or outside dialogue, and anywhere in a sentence. By now, you should be able to understand the second expression.

## *Alternate method*

If you have more time, you may want to perform the previous searches with increased scope, finding all contractions involving **'d** or **'s** or **'ve**, no matter what the contracted word. To do this, simply search, with or without wildcards enabled, for: **'d, 's, 've, 'd've, 're,** and **'ll**. Perform a separate search for each one. You will have many more hits that those revealed by the more focused previous search.

> "Simplicity is the most difficult thing to secure in this world; it is the last limit of experience and the last effort of genius."                —George Sand.

# Remove Redundancies

The previous searches dealt with the danger of too little information, a side effect of using vague and ambiguous words. The present search targets just the opposite—too much information. The list on the next page is provided to make you think about similar phrases you may have included in you manuscript—two or more words that mean the same thing where a single word will suffice.

When the reader is force-fed too much information, particularly information that is repetitive, he or she will quickly tire from the act of reading.

For an explanation of some of the phrases, read the rest of this paragraph while referring to the list. *Adequate* is always *enough* so one of those words is redundant. *Planning* is always done in *advance*; *essentials* are always *basic*; *close* refers to *proximity* (*proximity* is unneeded); a *consensus* is a form of *opinion*; it is impossible to *cooperate* alone; *decisions* are always *definite*; *elongated* refers to *length*; *unique* is the extreme aspect of difference; *gifts* are always *free*; *history* always refers to the *past*; and *facts* are always *true*.

I hope these examples will give you some ideas about what to search for in your manuscript.

## 43) Removal of Redundancies

**Comment:** As with other lists in this book, cross out the terms you know that you never use so that you do not waste time searching for them. The words with an asterisk have appeared on at least one other list in the book so far. Consequently, if you have performed all the searches up until this point, you can skip those. If you haven't, consider those to be slightly more objectionable than the others.

A. Disable "Use wildcards" and switch from Replace mode to Find mode (use the tabs)

B. *Find what:* [terms from the list of "Redundancies"]

   *Replace with:* [empty] The "Replace with" field will not be visible in Find mode.

C. Selectively search: Use **Cmd+G** (Apple) or **Ctrl+Alt+Y** (Windows) and revise as required.

## Redundancies

| | | |
|---|---|---|
| absolutely essential | famous celebrities | outside periphery |
| absolutely necessary | final destination | past history |
| added bonus | first priority | prior history |
| adequate enough | foreseeable future | postponed until later |
| advance planning | free gift | protective armor |
| advance warming | freezing cold | rate of speed |
| and also | frozen tundra | resemble in appearance |
| appear to be | future predictions | round circle |
| appears to be | general rule | safe haven |
| bare naked | green colored | safe sanctuary |
| basic essentials | green in color | same exact |
| brief moment | honest truth | spinning around |
| circle around | hot water heater | small speck |
| close proximity | humanitarian aid | smile happily |
| completely filled | income coming in | still remains |
| completely unanimous | increase in increments | tall skyscraper |
| consensus of opinion | immortalized forever | terrible tragedy |
| cooperated together | individual person | totally unique |
| dark night | initial prototype | true facts |
| definite decision | initial model | twelve in number |
| duplicate copy | joint cooperation | undisclosed        secret |
| each and every * | major breakthrough | location |
| elongated in length | merge together | unexpected surprise |
| empty space | modern science of today | unmarried bachelor |
| end result | most optimum | unprecedented new |
| evil villain | near vicinity | untimely death |
| exactly the same | necessary requirement | usual rule |
| exact same | new discovery | vast majority |
| exact replica | other alternatives | very unique |
| extremely unique | | |

# Banish the Boring

Boring words produce boring prose. The following list contains words that are often found in boring passages. While you probably cannot cut all occurrences of every one of these words from your manuscript, the more you cut, the more you will reduce the boring coefficient in your writing.

If you have time, consider performing this search after first crossing out the ones you know that you never use. There are about 60 words in this list, so if you spend an average of two minutes searching for each one, which will give you some time to delete or replace them, you will require about two hours.

## 44) Banish the Boring

**Comment:** As with other lists in this book, cross out the terms you know you never use so that you do not waste time searching for them. The words with an asterisk have appeared on at least one other list in the book so far. Consequently, if you have performed all the searches up until this point, you can skip those. If you haven't, consider those to be slightly more objectionable than the others.

---

A. Disable "Use wildcards" and switch from Replace mode to Find mode (use the tabs)

B. *Find what:* [terms from the list of "Boring Words"]

*Replace with:* [empty] The "Replace with" field will not be visible in Find mode.

C. Selectively search: Use **Cmd+G** (Apple) or **Ctrl+Alt+Y** (Windows) and revise as required.

---

The list of Boring Words appears on the following page.

## Potentially Boring Words

| | | |
|---|---|---|
| absolutely | exactly * | presently |
| accordingly | fairly * | probably |
| actually * | finally * | quite * |
| almost * | frequently | really * |
| amazing | fully | respective * |
| anxiously | fundamentally | respectively |
| approximately * | highly * | seemingly * |
| basically * | hopefully | simply * |
| certainly | incessantly | slightly * |
| completely | incredibly | successive * |
| constantly | ironically | suddenly |
| continually | literally | surprisingly |
| continuously | merely | totally |
| currently | mostly * | truly * |
| eagerly | nearly * | unfortunately |
| entire * | numerous | utterly * |
| entirely | obviously | very * |
| equally | only | wholly |
| especially | personally | wonderful |
| essentially | practically * | wonderfully |
| eventually | predictably | |

# Plunder Plague Words

My advice to you concerning the plague word list is the same as that for the boring word list. If you have time, consider performing this search after first crossing out the ones you know that you never use. There are less than 100 in this list, so if you spend an average of two minutes searching for each one, which will give you some time to delete or replace them, you will require about three-and-a-half hours.

Plague word lists abound on the Internet. The one I have assembled has evolved over a period of ten years, and I cannot recall where the original list came from. A related list is Lake Superior State University's annual Banish Words List. You can find the words that have been banished (usually because of overuse) during the current year at www.lssu.edu/banished.

Previous lists, going back to 1976, can be found here: www.lssu.edu/banished/archived_lists.php, and the most recent complete list in alphabetical order, noting the year of banishment, can be found here:

http://www.lssu.edu/banished/complete_list.php

## 44) **Plunder Plague Words**

**Comment:** As with other lists in this book, cross out the terms you know you never use so that you do not waste time searching for them. The words with an asterisk have appeared on at least one other list in the book so far. Consequently, if you have performed all the searches up until this point, you can skip those. If you haven't, consider those to be slightly more objectionable than the others.

---

A. Disable "Use wildcards" and switch from Replace mode to Find mode (use the tabs)

B. *Find what:* [terms from the list of "Plague Words"]

   *Replace with:* [empty] The "Replace with" field will not be visible in Find mode.

C. Selectively search: Use **Cmd+G** (Apple) or **Ctrl+Alt+Y** (Windows) and revise as required.

---

The list of Plague Words appears on the following page.

## Plague Words

| | | |
|---|---|---|
| absolutely * | impacted | prioritize |
| aforesaid | implement | productivity |
| and/or | individual | quite * |
| appall | infomercial | rather * |
| appalling | initial | real |
| apparently | input | reality-based |
| attempt | insightful | re-engineering |
| attitude | instantiation | reinventing |
| bi-partisanship | instantiate | remainder |
| bots | instantiated | repository |
| brainstorming | instantiating | respective * |
| branding | interesting | revisit |
| burgeoning | interface | robust |
| conceptualization | irregardless | scenario |
| conceptualize | irrespective | secondly |
| cyber | issues | seems * |
| disenfranchise | just * | segue |
| diva | leverage | self-starter |
| do-able | literal | self-titled |
| dot.com | lots | sketchy |
| dotcom | macho | skyrocket |
| dot-com | meaningful | so-called |
| dude | mean-spirited | solidarity |
| emote | medaled | spearhead |
| enormity | medication | spearheaded |
| enthuse | millennium | state-of-the-art |
| even * | multi-tasking | sucks |
| ever | myself | sufficient |
| experiencing | nature | synergy |
| extreme | nauseous | thirdly |
| facilitate | necessitate | thru |
| factoid | nine-eleven | too |
| factor | no-brainer | tortuous |
| fashionista | notables | torturous |
| firstly | numerous * | transpire |
| flat-out | obviously * | transpired |
| forewarn | offload | try |
| frankly | off-sourcing | ubiquitous |
| frig | oftentimes | underscored |
| frigging | ofttimes | unplugged |
| functionality | online | upscale |
| gifting | orientate | utilization |
| got | orientating | utilize |
| gotten | out-sourcing | very * |
| greats | parenting | viable |
| gutsy | patriate | virtually |
| he/she | patriation | whatever |
| heads-up | per | whatsup |
| hello!? | personalize | winningest |
| high-tech | previous | world-class |
| hi-tech | | Y2K |

# Chapter Ten

# Advanced Searches

## Search for Nominalizations and Gerunds

This section is titled "Advanced Searches" because the searches require more knowledge than the earlier searches in this book. So far, none of the searches have required that you know very much about grammar; these final searches do have that requirement.

Besides requiring basic knowledge of grammar, the advanced searches may be more time-consuming than the searches up until this point. Therefore, these carry the same warning as the last two searches in the previous section ("Banish the Boring" and "Plague Words"): you may want to skip these searches if you are trying to finish your final edit in less that 12 hours. On the other hand, if you do have the time to polish every facet of the jewel that is your manuscript, by all means, go for it!

> "No dependent clauses, no dangling things, no flashbacks, and keeping the subject near the predicate. We throw in as many fresh words as we can get away with. Simple, short sentences don't always work. You have to do tricks with pacing, alternate long sentences with short, to keep it vital and alive. Virtually every page is a cliffhanger—you've got to force them to turn it."
> —Theodore Seuss Geisel (Dr. Seuss)

## 46) Target Nominalizations

**Comment:** Nominalizations are verbs or adjectives that have been converted to nouns, usually by adding a suffix. The most common suffix for this purpose is *-ing*, but there are at least 40 others.

The *-ing* present participle form of the verb, sometimes called the participle noun, is more commonly known as a gerund. When a gerund is preceded by a noun or pronoun, it should be in possessive form.

To improve a sentence that includes a nominalization or gerund, convert the word back into the verb or adjective from which it was created. Always keep in mind that not all nominalizations and gerunds are bad.

---

A. Enable "Use wildcards" and switch from Replace mode to Find mode (use the tabs)

B. Find what: **([a-z]ing)([^32.,"—...'\?\!])**

   *Replace with:* [empty] The "Replace with" field will not be visible in Find mode.

C. Selectively search: Use **Cmd+G** (Apple) or **Ctrl+Alt+Y** (Windows) and revise as required.

---

**Explanation:** The "Find what" targets any word that ends in the suffix **–ing**, no matter where it comes in a sentence. It does this by ensuring that the letter before the **-ing** is a vowel **[a-z]**, and that anything coming after the **–ing** is not a letter (**[^32.,"—...'\?\!]**).

**Variation:** Here is a complete list of nominalization suffixes, but searching for all these will be time-consuming and may be unnecessary unless you are aware that you have a problem with nominalization. To perform this search, substitute each suffix on the following list for the **ing** that is in the first expression of the "Find what" field in the main search.

acy, age, al, ama, ana, ance, ant, dom, edge, ee, eer, er, ery, ese, ess, ette, fest, ful, hood, iac, ian, ie, y, ion, ism, ist, ite, itude, ity, ium, let, ling, man, mania, ment, ness, or, ship, th, tude,

## 47) Target Adverbs Ending in "ly"

**Comment:** Adverbs modify verbs, adjectives, other adverbs, clauses, and entire sentences. Most writing will be improved by reducing the number of adverbs. The most objectionable adverbs are those that modify verbs; they "add" additional meaning to the "verb," hence the word "adverb."

Sometimes, writers use adverbs to modify verbs when they cannot think of the right verb to use in context or they do not have time to stop and think about the problem.

Example: *They spoke very quietly.* The word "spoke" is the verb, "quietly" is an adverb modifying "spoke," and "very" is an adverb modifying "quietly." This is a case in which the writer forgot the word "whispered." *They whispered* would have been a much better way to express the same thing.

Adverbs add the following shades of meaning to the word that they modify: *when, where, how, why, in what way, to what extent or to what degree (how much), how often,* and *under what conditions.*

The vast majority of adverbs end in the suffix *-ly*, so searching for words ending in that suffix should reveal more than half of the adverbs in your manuscript.

**Four things to pay special attention to during this search:**

1) Adverbs that modify an attribution verb are particularly disruptive, so closely monitor such adverbs revealed by this search. When your search reveals such usages you should change the attribution or delete the adverb and add a non-adverbial tag to the attribution that communicates the same meaning.

2) Usually, sentence adverbs are single words that end in *–ly*, and a comma always follows these adverbs. Consequently, during this search, make sure that a comma follows any sentence adverbs that turn up. Incidentally, "Usually" in the first sentence of this paragraph, "consequently" in the previous sentence, and "incidentally," in this sentence are sentence adverbs. The word "consequently" is a special type of adverb called a "conjunctive adverb." This means the adverb creates a link to the previous sentence. It is still a sentence adverb so a comma must follow it.

3) "Squinting modifiers" are adverbs (sometimes comprising entire phrases) that are ambiguous. Remember the effects of ambiguity described in the introduction to search #42b? The reader can understand squinting modifiers as modifying either the word or phrase they follow or the word or phrase they precede. Example: "Deciphering the squinting modifiers of those who were writing *quickly* caused the teacher to throw up his hands in despair." Does the sentence concern "those who were *writing quickly*" or that they "*quickly caused* the teacher to throw up his hands"?

4) Certain dangling phrases (A.K.A. "danglers") begin with an adverb ending in -ly. Example: *Obliviously combining* adverb upon adverb, *the sentences* of his novel filled page after page. (Italics have been added to indicate the culprits.) This dangler has the sentences of a novel itself combining adverb upon adverb. That sounds like a good way for an author to disavow accountability for his poor grammar ("It wasn't me, Your Honor, all the adverbial abuse in my novel was committed by the sentences, themselves!")

Other adverb suffixes exist. If you have a problem with adverbs, you should search for them. The following search targets words ending in the suffix *-ly* because such words are usually adverbs.

---

A.  Enable "Use wildcards" and switch from Replace mode to Find mode (use the tabs)

B.  *Find what:* **([a-z]ly)([^32.," — …'\?\!])**
    note: *If you performed the variation of Search #27 then substitute* **([a-z]ly)([.," — …'\?\!])**

    *Replace with:* [empty] The "Replace with" field will not be visible in Find mode.

C.  Selectively search: Use **Cmd+G** (Apple) or **Ctrl+Alt+Y** (Windows) and revise as required.

---

**False positives:** Some false positives are possible with this search because some words ending in *-ly* are not adverbs. Examples: *family, fly*

## 48a) Reflexive Pronouns vs. Nominative and Objective Pronouns

**Comment:** Perhaps television, Hollywood, untrained writers, or a combination of the three have brought an utterly disagreeable habit to the world, that is, the substitution of the reflexive pronoun "myself" for the personal pronouns "I" and "me." No matter what the cause, this is unacceptable!

Examples: My agent and *myself* met with the editor. The editor had a lengthy meeting with my agent and *myself*. The first example should have "I" in place of "myself," and the second should have "me" instead of "myself." There are no exceptions to this rule.

Use this search to examine all occurrences of the word "myself" for this error.

A. Disable "Use wildcards" and switch from Replace mode to Find mode (use the tabs)

B. *Find what:* **myself**

   *Replace with:* [empty] The "Replace with" field will not be visible in Find mode.

C. Selectively search: Use **Cmd+G** (Apple) or **Ctrl+Alt+Y** (Windows) and delete or revise as appropriate.

**Allowable:** A reflexive pronoun used as an intensifier is acceptable. Example: "*Final Edit* enabled me to edit the entire final draft of my novel, *myself*." Use this test: The word "me" can never be substituted for a reflexive pronoun used as an intensifier.

## 48b) Nominative Case Pronouns vs. Objective Case Pronouns

**Comment:** Possibly related to the reflexive pronoun problem addressed by the previous search is the abhorrent use of objective case pronouns ("Him" or "Her") in places where the nominative case ("He" or "She") is required. No matter what the cause, this is unacceptable!

Examples: "Him and I went to the writers conference." "Her and her sister attended the critique group." The first example should have "He" in place of "Him," and the second should have "She" instead of "Her." There are no exceptions to this rule.

Use this search to examine all occurrences of the words "Him" or "Her" for this error.

> A.  Enable "Use wildcards" and switch from Replace mode to Find mode (use the tabs)
>
> B.  *Find what:* (**<H[ie][mr]>**)
>
>     *Replace with:* [empty] The "Replace with" field will not be visible in Find mode.
>
> C.  Selectively search: Use **Cmd+G** (Apple) or **Ctrl+Alt+Y** (Windows) and revise as appropriate.

**False positives:** Inspirational texts that use a capitalized "Him" as the objective pronoun for the deity will be revealed by this search.

## Passive, levels of time, appositives, non-restrictive phrases, and more

Avoid passive voice; use active voice instead. You've probably heard this ever since the first day you showed your writing to a person who could distinguish between the two. Passive voice occurs when the object of a sentence becomes the subject (and vice versa). While it is not possible to target all forms of passive voice, our trusty Find & Replace box can detect several patterns that often occur in passive voice constructions.

The progenitor search string from which the others are derived is as follows:

$$([Ii]t^32is^32)(<[a-z][a-z]\{1,2\}ed>)$$

The first expression resolves to "It is " and "it is " (Note the trailing space after the is.) The second expression resolves to any word that begins with a lowercase letter that is followed by two more letters before ending with "ed" (Did you catch the "followed by two more letters?") There appears to be a bug in Word that will not accept a true range in subsequent bracketed range indicators like this, although the first bracketed range indicator functions as expected.

This search string will find "It is " or "it is " followed by a 5 letter word, the last two letters of which are "ed." To find a six-letter word, you need to change the final "2" to a "3"; for a seven-letter word, change it to a "4"; for and eight-letter word, change it to a "5"; and so forth (the "ed" counts as 2 letters). It's a good idea to continue this progression until you have changed that final number to "9" to detect words in the past tense with up to 12 characters.

Example: *The computer program was written by a musician.* This sentence is in passive voice. *A musician wrote the computer program* would be a much better way to state this because it recasts the sentence in active voice.

See the comments of the following searches to understand the evolution of this progenitor search string.

## 49a) Target Possible Passive Voice

**Comment:** Although these searches will not come near to detecting all occurrences of passive voice, they will find some cases. Any reduction in passive voice will enhance your manuscript; the more, the better.

This search targets the first ten of the following patterns. The final two (in parentheses) can be accomplished by way of common, no wildcard searches for "could have been," "might have been," and "will have been."

### Possible Passive Voice

| | |
|---|---|
| is/are *verbed* | will be *verbed* |
| is/are being *verbed* | will have been *verbed* |
| was/were *verbed* | to be *verbed* |
| was/were being *verbed* | to have been *verbed* |
| has/had/have been *verbed* | (could have been *verbed*) |
| can be *verbed* | (might have been *verbed*) |

**Remember:** Because of the bug in some versions of Word, you may need to increment the final digit in the final expression from 2 through 9. In such cases, this creates eight searches for each search string—a total of sixteen searches.

A. Enable "Use wildcards" and switch from Replace mode to Find mode (use the tabs)

B. *Find what:* [First perform the 3-word version, then the 4-word version.]

3-word version (Character name or any capitalized noun or lowercase personal pronoun followed by an auxiliary, ending with a verb+ed)

**(<[A-Zwiths][a-z]{1,15}>)(^32)([wiha][reads]{1,3})¬ (^32)(<[a-z][a-z]{1,2}ed>)**

4-word version (Character name or any capitalized noun or lowercase personal pronoun followed by 2 auxiliaries, ending with a verb+ed

**(<[A-Zwiths][a-z]{1,15}>)(^32)([wihact][readson]{1,3})¬ (^32)(b[eing]{1,4})(^32)(<[a-z][a-z]{1,2}ed>)**

*Replace with:* [empty] The "Replace with" field will not be visible in Find mode.

C. Selectively search: Use **Cmd+G** (Apple) or **Ctrl+Alt+Y** (Windows) and revise as appropriate.

**False positives:** These searches produce very few false positives.

## 49b) Target Extraneous Past Perfect

**Comment**: This search targets occurrences of "had." You will check whether the found instances of "had" are part of a past perfect construction ("He *had checked* for past perfect constructions"). Then, look around the context to validate other nearby uses of the past perfect. The first "had" brings us into the past; for example, to a flashback. Everything following that initial signal (the first sentence or clause in the past perfect) is one level deeper into the past, so you can use the simple past for the entire section; that is, until you want to go deeper into the past (backstory within a flashback, for example) or return to the present. At the end of the section that is further in the past than the main story, a closing simple perfect sentence or clause brings the reader back to the level of time prior to the opening had.

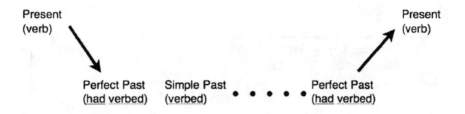

Alternatively, once you have entered the past by way of a single sentence (or clause) in past perfect, and have continued for a while with the simple past, you can force the next past perfect sentence (or clause) to jump a level deeper into the past by, for example, using a sentence adverb that makes clear the temporal direction indicated by the past perfect signal.

Example: "*Earlier*, the lamb *had followed* Mary to school." *Earlier* informs the reader that the subsequent past perfect will take us deeper into the past and not back to the present. In this scenario two past perfect sentences or clauses are usually required to orient the reader back to the present; the first takes the reader back to the time-period of the initial flashback, and the second takes us back to the present.

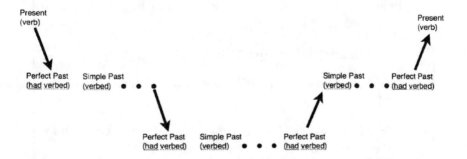

The search for extraneous uses of the past perfect targets capitalized character names up to 16 characters long, capitalized pronouns, and lowercase pronouns followed by a space and then the word "had."

A.  Enable "Use wildcards" and switch from Replace mode to Find mode (use the tabs)

B.  *Find what:* **(<[A-Zwiths][a-z]{1,15}>)(^32had)**

*Replace with:* [empty] The "Replace with" field will not be visible in Find mode.

C.  Selectively search: Use **Cmd+G** (Apple) or **Ctrl+Alt+Y** (Windows) and revise as appropriate.

**False positives:** These searches produce very few false positives.

## 49c) Target Second Word in Sentence = "had" or "was"

**Comment**: Several chapters ago, we targeted paragraph starters and sentence starters that included "is" or "was" as the second word (searches #30a, b, and c, and #31a, b, and c). This present search is similar, but of much wider scope: Any words, capitalized or not, followed by "had" or "was" will be revealed.

A.  Enable "Use wildcards" and switch from Replace mode to Find mode (use the tabs)

B.  *Find what:* **(<[A-Z][a-z]{1,15}>)(^32)([hw]a[ds])**

*Replace with:* [empty] The "Replace with" field will not be visible in Find mode.

C.  Selectively search: Use **Cmd+G** (Apple) or **Ctrl+Alt+Y** (Windows) and revise as appropriate.

## 49d) Target Second Word in Sentence = "seemed" or "appeared"

**Comment**: Several chapters ago, we targeted paragraph starters and sentence starters that included "is" or "was" as the second word (searches #30a, b, and c, and #31a, b, and c). This current search is similar, but of much wider scope: Any words, capitalized or not, followed by "seemed" or "appeared" will trigger a hit.

> A. Enable "Use wildcards" and switch from Replace mode to Find mode (use the tabs)
>
> B. *Find what:* **(<[A-Z][a-z]{1,15}>)(^32)([sa][pream]{3,5}ed)**
>
> *Replace with:* [empty] The "Replace with" field will not be visible in Find mode.
>
> C. Selectively search: Use **Cmd+G** (Apple) or **Ctrl+Alt+Y** (Windows) and revise as appropriate.

**Caveat:** Because of the Word bug mentioned earlier in this chapter, the fact that there are two bracketed range indications means that the second one might not function correctly. You may need to perform this search twice, the first time with a "5" as the last number of the last bracketed range, and the second time with "4" as the last number. Alternatively, you could execute the search once with "seemed" as the final expression, and a second time with "appeared" as the final expression. Either way, it is two searches.

## Final Edit's Final Search

We have reached the final search in our final edit. Although this search might not seem as complicated as #49a, the grammar issues are beyond any that have been addressed so far. For this search you will need to understand nonrestrictive appositives and nonrestrictive phrases and clauses.

Because restrictive appositives, phrases, and clauses do not require commas and nonrestrictive appositives do require commas, you must understand the meaning of the words "restrictive" and "nonrestrictive" when they are used in this context. Although many highfaluting explanations of the two terms exist, I find it is easiest to think of restrictive as indicating *required information*, and nonrestrictive as indicating *optional information*. Another way to look at these terms is that they indicate whether certain information is *essential* or *non-essential* to comprehending the meaning of the word(s) they follow.

An appositive can be a single word or an entire phrase or clause. It follows a noun on noun phrase, and identifies, explains, or otherwise describes the noun or noun phrase by conveying additional information about it. This additional information can be either restrictive (required or essential to the comprehension of the text), or nonrestrictive (optional or non-essential to the comprehension of the text). It can occur within a sentence (intra-sentence) or at the end of a sentence.

Nonrestrictive appositives within a sentence require a pair of commas; those at the end of sentences require a single comma; the terminal punctuation takes the place of the second comma.

A pair of commas in fiction can function in the same way as parentheses in non-fiction (parentheses are not used in fiction). In other words, a pair of commas can surround a nonrestrictive appositive, or they can surround any other parenthetical statement consisting of a nonrestrictive phrase or clause. A pair of em dashes can be used for the latter purpose—as a parenthetical statement—in either fiction or non-fiction, but em dashes are used to delineate appositives only when the appositive involves a comma-delimited list. You may recall that em dashes have other uses, too, and these were described in the chapter about problematic punctuation.

The presence or absence of an article or possessive pronoun before the noun or noun phrase preceding the appositive sometimes can be used to determine whether this appositive is restrictive or nonrestrictive and therefore, whether it requires commas.

> His sergeant, Hans Feldwebel, required that they wake up at 4 AM.

> The sergeant, Hans Feldwebel, required that they wake up at 4 AM.

> Sergeant Hans Feldweble required that they wake up at 4 AM.

Without the article or possessive pronoun, the appositive is usually restrictive.

If you can delete the appositive without changing the sense of the passage, the appositive is nonrestrictive (i.e., non-essential). Try doing so in the following examples:

> The editor of the Daily Planet, Perry White, could not have known Superman's secret identity.

> Those who could not have know Superman's secret identity included the editor of the Daily Planet, Perry White.

While considering the hits revealed by the following searches, you should keep in mind that another usage of a pair of commas or a closing comma-delimited segment is called an interjection. For example, the phrases "of course" and "indeed" are often an interjection.

> He could have edited his manuscript without using the tools provided by *Final Edit*, of course, but then it would have required another four weeks of his life.

> He could have hired a professional editor, of course, but the expense would have been astronomical considering the length of his manuscript.

## 50) Target Nonrestrictive Appositives, Phrases, and Clauses

**Comments:** The first three groups of searches target the comma phrase according to its location: 1) an internal passage enclosed but a pair of commas, 2) the opening component of the sentence is followed by a comma, or 3) the closing component of the sentence begins after a comma (the final comma is effectively replaced by the terminal punctuation).

The fourth group of searches targets all locations of comma phrases, regardless of their location, except as indicated in the explanatory notes.

Each of these four groups is further broken down into one to three search strings: 1) the search string targets comma phrases that begin with a capitalized word (e.g., a character name), 2) the search string targets comma phrases that begin with a lowercase word, and 3) the search string targets all comma phrases, regardless of whether they begin with a capital letter or not. These searches are all selective searches.

| Internal passages enclosed by a pair of commas | |
|---|---|
| (, )(<[A-Z]*[a-z]>[,]) | Begins with a capital letter |
| (, )(<[a-z]*[a-z]>[,]) | Begins with a lowercase letter |
| (, )(<[A-Z]*[a-z]>[,]) | Begins with either of the two |

| Opening component of sentence is followed by a comma | |
|---|---|
| ([^13^32\"])(<[A-Z]*[a-z]>[,]) | Begins with a capital letter |

| Closing component of sentence begins with a comma | |
|---|---|
| (, )(<[A-Z]*[a-z]>[:;.'" — ...\?\!]) | Begins with a capital letter |
| (, )(<[a-z]*[a-z]>[:;.'" — ...\?\!]) | Begins with a lowercase letter |
| (, )(<[A-Z]*[a-z]>[:;.'" — ...\?\!]) | Begins with either of the two |

| Search for all of the above with a single search | |
|---|---|
| ([^13,^32]{1,2})¬<br>(<[A-Z]*[a-z]>[:;.,'" — ...\?\!]) | Any location; beginning with a capital letter |
| (, )(<[a-z]*[a-z]>[:;.,'" — ...\?\!]) | Any location; beginning with a lowercase letter |
| (, )(<[A-z]*[a-z]>[:;.,'" — ...\?\!]) | Any location; beginning with a lowercase letter |

The third search in the fourth group will target all comma phrases except those at the beginning of a paragraph, no matter their location or capitalization. This search will result in the most hits—all the hits of the other searches, combined.

> A. Enable "Use wildcards" and switch from Replace mode to Find mode (use the tabs)
>
> B. *Find what:* [Choose search strings from the preceding table.]
>
> *Replace with:* [empty] The "Replace with" field will not be visible in Find mode.
>
> C. Selectively search: Use **Cmd+G** (Apple) or **Ctrl+Alt+Y** (Windows) and revise as appropriate.

**False positives:** These searches can produce false positives; however, the false positives are easy to recognize because they usually cross sentence or paragraph boundaries.

# Use Your Imagination

By now, you should be able to accomplish whatever you can imagine by way of the Find & Replace box (within the limits that are set by the programmers of Word). It is time to use your imagination and create your own custom searches for the final polishing of your draft, searches designed to fix problems unique to your draft or writing style, idiosyncratic problems that were not addressed by the searches in this book. Some examples follow.

**Example 1: Problems with Italics.** Do you have a problem with italics? You now know that you can easily search for italicized passages simply by placing the cursor in the (empty) "Find what" field and selecting "Font..." from the "Formatting" popup menu. In the "Font" dialog box, enter "Italic" in the "Font style" field either by typing the word or selecting it from the scrolling list below. Without enabling wildcards, perform a selective search. Each hit will be an entire italicized passage.

You need to remember the rules: Use italics for the titles of large works, book titles, movies, operas, musicals, ballets, plays, magazines, newspapers, but use quotation marks for the titles of articles, essays, poems, short stories, paintings, sculptures, TV series, and songs. Also, use italics for "interior monologue." For example: *I wonder if I included the "interior monologue" section...*

**Example 2: Non-Capitalized Days of the Week.** Do you worry that you might have typed a day of the week without capitalizing it? You could perform seven searches, one for each day in lowercase, with "Case sensitive" enabled in the Find & Replace box. But, because you now understand wildcards, you can accomplish the same result by way of a single search with wildcards enabled and the following search string: **[smtwf][a-z]{2,5}day**

The **smtwf** means the word must begin with one of those letters; the **[a-z]** is followed by the bracketed limits of **2** to **5** occurrences of those lowercase letters; the expression ends with the syllable **day**; all lowercased days of the week will be revealed.

**Example 3: All Caps Indicates Shouting.** Passages in all caps are used to indicate shouting, words run together (when used without spaces), or to add emphasis. Some book designers capitalize the first 1 to 5 words or the entire first lines of chapters. Do you worry that you may have passages in all caps that do not honor those rules? The following search string will find all capitalized passages.

**[^13^32\"][A-Z][A-Z]{1,9}[\?\!.,'" — …^32^13]**

**Example 4: Former Article Remains After Change of Noun.** One repeated error made by many writers is forgetting to delete the former article when a changed or revised noun requires a different article. All permutations of the errors "a an," "a the," and "the an" are common. If you have this problem, search for all two-word combinations of *a, an,* and *the* surrounded by spaces.

**space+an+space+a+space**
**space+a+space+an+space**
**space+a+space+the+space**
**space+the+space+a+space**
**space+an+space+the+space**
**space+the+space+an+space**

**Example 5: An or an Followed by a Vowel.** Your personal error might be following the article "an" with a word starting with a vowel. The following search will find all such cases:

**(^32[Aa]n^32)([!][aeiouaeiou])**

**Example 6: Commonly Confused Words.** Every writer has some words that he or she confuses. Examples of words that are often confused appear on the following table.

### Commonly Confused Words

| | |
|---|---|
| accept and except | illicit and elicit |
| adverse and averse | immigrate and emigrate |
| affect and effect | imminent and eminent |
| all together and altogether | instinctive, not instinctual |
| among, not amongst | its and it's |
| anticipate and expect | led and lead |
| any more and anymore | lets and let's |
| anytime or any time | literally and figuratively |
| before, not prior to or previous to | moot point, not mute point |
| can and may | nauseous and nauseated |
| childish and childlike | person, not individual |
| continuous and continual | phenomena and phenomenon |
| convince and persuade | presently, not currently |
| could have, not could of | principle and principal |
| criteria and criterion | purposely and purposefully |
| differing and different | recur and reoccur |
| disinterested and uninterested | then and than |
| eager and anxious | there, they're, and their |
| ensure and assure | try to, not try and |
| for a while, not for awhile | used to, not use to |
| further and farther | whether, not as to whether |
| hanged and hung | who and whom |
| historic and historical | whose and who's |

What are your problem word pairs? Make a list and search for each of them. It will help to have a usage reference while you perform this search. The first three books about usage in Appendix II "Books About Writing" cover commonly confused word pairs, each with more examples than the previous.

**Example 7: Comma-delineated List Problems.** A serious error occurs when a comma does not follow the item preceding the "and" or "or" in a comma-delineated list of three or more items; that is, unless the final two items are designated as a sub-group the list. Unfortunately, Word does not make it easy to search for such problems; however, we can search for instances of "and" and "or" that are not preceded by a comma. This will turn up many false positives because two items connected by "and" or "or" do not require a comma.

Search for: **[!\,](^32and)** to find cases involving "and," and search for **[!\,](^32or)** to find cases involving "or."

## Chapter Eleven

# Final Steps

## Final Steps

You will need to take a few more steps to make your file ready for your book designer (even if you are the book designer), for eBook conversion, or before you submit it to an agent or publisher. However, having just completed the *Final Edit* process, your manuscript is in much better shape to make these required changes and you will probably be able to finish this task in less than an hour.

If you haven't assigned styles yet, your manuscript is now ready for styles.

## Introduction to Styles

Styles were introduced in the "Recommendations" section of the chapter title "Essential Setup" and also in the chapter about initial words in paragraphs and sentences.

The beauty of styles is that you can change the look of an element once (for example, the size, font, and spacing of your body text) and this will change all other body text in your book, provided it has been assigned the *Body Text* style. Using styles will save your book designer and eBook conversion service many hours and possibly, many days. This should save you many dollars.

Most of your text will use a *Body Text* style, and you may require a *Block Quotation* style (for text indented from both right and left margins). Chapter titles and subheads will also require separate styles. If your work has figures, you may need a *Caption* style for the captions.

You may want specific styles for your *Frontal-Matter Headings*, or simply use your *Chapter Title* style. Some manuscripts will require a *Chapter Subtitle* style and one or more levels of *Headings* and *Sub-Heading* styles. If your book uses numbered or bulleted lists (or both), those should be assigned *Numbered List* or *Bulleted List* styles.

Another style that most books required is an indented body text style for the first sentence in each chapter. You might name this *Body Text No Indent* or *First Paragraph.* Other common styles are the *Footer* and *Header* styles. If you have different right and left footers and headers, you will require *Footer Left, Footer Right, Header Left,* and *Header Right* styles. You might want to name these *Footer Even, Footer Odd, Header Even,* and *Header Odd* because odd-numbered pages are always on the right.

Depending upon the complexity of your document, you may need a *Footnote* style and a style for *Citations* in your bibliography.

Any element that appears more than once and that is a member of a class of similar elements should have its own style. However, styles should be used in moderation. Never confuse things by making multiple shades of *Body Text* or *Chapter Titles.*

The recommended **List of Basic Styles** on the next page is simply an example. Your manuscript might not require Chapter Subtitles; it might not even require Chapter Titles because you use only Chapter Numbers. The schema works well for eBook conversion, too.

| List of Basic Styles | |
| --- | --- |
| **Style name** | **Default Next Style** |
| Title | Subtitle |
| Subtitle | Author |
| Author | Copyright |
| Copyright | Chapter Title |
| Chapter Title | Chapter Subtitle |
| Chapter Subtitle | Chapter Number |
| Chapter Number | Body |
| Body | Body |
| Body Bullet List | |
| Body Numbered List | |
| Heading | Body |
| Heading Alternate | Body |
| Subheading | Body |
| Subheading Alternate | Body |
| Block Quote | |
| Caption | Body |
| Footnote Text | |
| Header (Even) | |
| Header (Odd) | |
| Footer (Even) | |
| Footer (Odd) | |

### *Define Before you Assign*

While you design your styles, keep in mind that most of them should be "Paragraph Styles" instead of "Character Styles." Usually, Character Styles are reserved for footnote references and page numbers. You might name such styles *Footnote references* and *Page numbers.*

Define styles by selecting text that you have formatted to be the way you want it to look, and then press the "New Style" button on the "Formatting" palette, or select "Style..." from the "Format" menu. If you have manually formatted the selected text before entering the "Style" dialog box, about all you will have to do is give your new style a name. Because most of your styles will be Paragraph Styles, you may want to choose "Paragraph..." from the "Format" popup menu at the bottom of the "Style" dialog box and adjust certain characteristics such as "Keep lines together," "Keep with next," "Widow/Orphan control," and "Page break before" (good for *Chapter Title* styles), for example. Before clicking "OK" in the Style dialog box, choose a "Style for following paragraph:" from its popup menu to specify what style you want to activate after you type in one style and press return to start a new paragraph. For your *Chapter Title* style, you probably want this set to *Body Text* or *Chapter Subtitle*. Other suggestions are provided in the right column of the previous table "List of Basic Styles."

Alternatively, you might use one of Word's pre-defined styles and alter it to your liking; then, on the "Pick style to apply" list in the "Formatting" palette, click on the ¶ symbol next to the name of the current style, and choose "Update style to match selection" from the ensuing popup menu.

It's that simple. But if you would like to learn about styles in greater detail, some excellent online Word Style Tutorials are provided in the Link List Appendix at the back of this book.

Of course, it would have saved time if you had set up your styles before you typed a single word, but I will assume that was not the case for the rest of this chapter. If your document is a mishmash of illogical styles, you might want to continue the following steps as if you had not assigned any styles.

If you are planning to self-publish or use a print-on-demand printer, once you have finished your final edit and have assigned your styles, your document is ready to be turned over to your book designer or eBook converter. You may play either or both of those roles, but if that is not the case, having the manuscript in the form it will be in after going through the *Final Edit* process, and after having pre-assigned styles should equate to substantial savings for those tasks.

## Style Assignment

After you have defined the styles you will need based upon the classes described above and in the previous table, you can assign the styles to the appropriate passages in your manuscript. Follow the two steps below to speed up this process.

Step 1)  Convert the entire document to *Body Text* ("Select All" then choose *Body Text* from the "Pick style to apply" list on the "Formatting" palette.)

Step 2)  Now assign your remaining styles. Because all or nearly all of your styles are paragraph styles, your cursor need merely be anywhere in the paragraph for the style to be assigned to the entire paragraph when you press the desired style name on the "Formatting" palette.

## Use Find & Replace to Automate Style Assignment

Your newly acquired knowledge of Word's Find & Replace box can automate the assignment of some styles. In fact, some styles can be assigned by way of a global replacement search with a single click.

If you have titled all your chapters so they commence with the word "Chapter" and you have not used the capitalized word "Chapter" anywhere else, you need simply search for the word **Chapter** (without formatting) and replace it with itself (the word **Chapter)** with the *Chapter Title* style already assigned (this will affect the chapter number, too). To do this, ensure that the word **Chapter** is in both the "Find what" and "Replace with" fields. Then, place cursor in the "Replace with" field and choose "Style…" from the "Format" popup menu at the lower left of the Find & Replace box. Choose the *Chapter Title* style from the ensuing popup list of your styles. Next, press the "Replace All" button. It's truly a one-click style assignment.

If you have used the word "Chapter" elsewhere in your manuscript, you may still be able to assign the *Chapter Title* style with a single click if you preceded each chapter title with a manual page break. If this is the case, simply search for **^mChapter** (a **manual page break** followed by the word **Chapter**) and proceed as in the previous paragraph. Incidentally, it's a very good idea to have all your chapter titles begin with the word "Chapter" because many software programs now expect your book to be set up that way so they can, for example, generate a linked TOC (Table of Contents).

Examine your document for other global style assignment possibilities, similar to the *Chapter Title* assignment described above. If you have started every figure caption with the word "Figure," then this could be another one-click assignment.

Similarly, if all your *Block Quotations* (indented from both left and right margins) begin with an open quotation mark and end with a **close quotation mark,** you can search for **(^13\"*\"^13)** and replace that with **\1** to which you have assigned the *Block Quotation* style. The "Find what" is a single expression that consists of a **return+open quotation mark+any** amount of **text+close quotation+return**. The "Replace with" is \1 (backslash+1), which means replace the found text with itself modified by any conditions assigned to the "Replace with" field (You will have assigned the style *Block Quotation* to this field in the same way you assigned *Chapter Title* to it in the earlier example. Note that if your manuscript is a novel, you should perform this search as a selective search because you may have some dialogue paragraphs that fulfill the conditions of this search. Alternatively, use your indented margins as the search target.

As mentioned in the "Recommendations" section of the chapter titled "Essential Setup," you may be tempted to leave each style set to 12-point Courier or Times because an agent or publisher has requested that your entire document be typed in that particular font or font size. Even if that is the case, you should still assign different, visually recognizable characteristics to each element because this will help you see, at a glance, which text has already been assigned a style and which is awaiting to be assigned a style. You can always save a copy of the document after having converted all the styles to 12-point Courier or Times as required; the agent or publisher receiving a printout of the manuscript will not be able to tell that the source document already had styles assigned.

## Tips for Writers Who Use Scrivener

Scrivener is a program developed by Literature and Latte specifically for writers. See the links to various versions of the program in Appendix I "Link List." There you will find links to the educational version at bit.ly/Scrivener-ed, the Macintosh version by way of bit.ly/Scrivener-Mac, and the Windows version by way of bit.ly/Scrivener-Win.

A common scenario among writers who use Scrivener is to write their books in Scrivener and then compile the manuscript into a file that can be brought into Word for its *Final Edit*. That is precisely how this book was written.

Having just touched upon the subject of how to "Use Find and Replace to Automate Style Assignment," I feel it is important to provide those readers who use Scrivener with some tips to leverage Scriveners "presets" so that the resulting compiled document can undergo automatic style assignment in Word.

The easiest way to do this is to make all your Scrivener presets unique in font size, font family, or both. Let's use font size as an example. In Scrivener (before compiling) assign a unique size to some text in each preset and then use Format → Formatting → Redefine Preset From Selection to assign that size to all occurrences of that preset.

Having done this, now you can use Word's Find & Replace box to convert everything of a specified font size to a designated Word style. Under the Find & Replace box's "Format" menu choose "Font…" then, with the cursor in the empty "Find what" field, specify the font size of a particular preset. Move the cursor to the "Replace with" field and choose the appropriate style from the "Style…" item at the bottom of the "Format" menu. Again, the field will be empty. Now press the "Replace All" button and everything of the chosen font size will be assigned to the same Word style.

It's a good idea keep the same font size that was used to identify the Scrivener preset as the font size of the destination Word style. After you have converted all your Scrivener presets to Word styles in this manner, it's a simple task to change the font sizes of the Word styles to whatever you prefer.

## Final Considerations

If you are your own book designer, you may want to assign characteristics to each style that will end up being the final design of the book.

On the other hand, if you will be submitting your manuscript to an agent or publisher, you should put the book in the format they request. If a single font and font size is required, with styles assigned, this is as simple as selecting all the text in your document and changing it to the requested size and font. Then, one by one, select text of each style name and proceed down the "Pick style to apply" list, choosing "Update to match selection" from that style's ¶ popup menu. Repeat for each style. It's best to save such one-font documents as a separate file, designated as intended for agents and publishers. Alternatively, create the single-font font version with "Select All" and the required font change without updating styles.

If you plan to do your own conversion to various eBook formats you should take a few more steps. First remove the headers and footers; eBooks don't have page numbers because you never know at what size the page will appear. Also remove page numbers from your table of contents because they have no meaning in the world of eBooks. An open-source (free) program like Calibre can save you time and money when you do your eBook conversion. Best of all, if you have done the edits described in this book and added styles, your conversion should go very smoothly.

Nonetheless, every book is unique so many eBook conversions require special formatting. If you convert your book to Kindle format and epub format, you will have covered the vast majority of eBook-readers. I recommend that you purchase the following books about eBook conversion if you have any problems:

***Kindle Formatting: The Complete Guide To Formatting Books For The Amazon Kindle*** by Joshua Tallent
> http://amzn.to/KindleFormatting

***EPUB Straight to the Point: Creating eBooks for the Apple iPad and other eBook-readers*** by Elizabeth Castro
> http://amzn.to/EPUBstraight

# Afterword

You've come a long way: from replacing multiple spaces with a single **space** to wild card searches such as #42b using expressions like ([^32^13\"])(^32)([TtWwhiaestnr]{4,5}'[dlre]{1,2}) to target complex word problems. Search #42b, you may recall, let you search for fifteen contracted words in three contexts. That is the 'd, 'll, and 're contraction forms of the words *this, that, what, when,* and *where.* The three contexts are 1) as the first word of a paragraph or internal sentence, 2) inside or outside dialogue, and 3) anywhere else in a sentence. That single search finds potential errors in 45 different ways (three contexts multiplied by fifteen contractions).

You have become an expert in wielding the full power of Word's Find & Replace box. You are able to reduce your editing time to a tiny fraction of what it has been up until now. You've saved thousands of dollars and hundreds of hours. More importantly, you can do it again and again, and each time you edit this way, you will become faster and more secure with the process. Moreover, in between editing your final drafts, your writing will improve because you now know how to produce prose that requires less editing during your final edit. The entire process will be faster each time.

Congratulations!

# APPENDIX I
# Link List

## Final Edit Website
ScienceOfWriting.com

## The Author's Websites
ChrisYavelow.com
FictionFixer.com
InterestingWriting.com

## Miscellaneous Links

**Scrivener**
Writing Software by Literature and Latte
(This book was written in Scrivener Mac, before
exporting the text to Word for its *Final Edit*. By the time
you read this Scrivener for Windows will be available.)

http://bit.ly/Scrivener-ed
http://bit.ly/Scrivener-Mac
http://bit.ly/Scrivener-Win

## The Editorial Freelancers Association
Rate List
http://www.the-efa.org/res/rates.php

## Banished Words Lists
Current "Banished Words" List
http://www.lssu.edu/banished.

Previous lists, by year, back to 1976
http://www.lssu.edu/banished/archived_lists.php

Complete list alphabetized
http://www.lssu.edu/banished/complete_list.php

# Word Help

## Help Setting Preferences
http://bit.ly/WordPrefs

## Word Help for Styles

Step-by-step explanation about creating Styles in Word 2010/2011
http://bit.ly/Styles2010-2011

Styles Video Tutorial: Word 2010/2011
http://bit.ly/StylesVideo2010-2011

Step-by-step explanation about creating Styles in Word 2010/2011
http://bit.ly/Styles2007-2008

Styles Video Tutorial: Word 2007/2008
http://bit.ly/StylesVideo2007-2008

## Word Help for Keyboard Shortcuts

Keyboard Shortcuts Step-by-step explanation
http://bit.ly/WordShortcuts

Keyboard Shortcuts Video Tutorial: 2010/2011
http://bit.ly/ShortcutsVideo2010-2011

Keyboard Shortcuts Video Tutorial: 2007-2008
http://bit.ly/ShortcutsVideo2007-2008

# APPENDIX 2
# Books About Writing

(Including amzn.to links)

This list is maintained at CraftOfWriting.com

A "Bitly Bundle" of these links is available at:
http://bit.ly/ScienceOfWritingLinks

## Fundamental Books about writing

### On Writing Well
William K. Zinsser
http://amzn.to/OnWritingWell

### The Art of Fiction
John Gardner
http://amzn.to/ArtOfFiction

### Stein on Writing
Sol Stein
http://amzn.to/SteinOnWriting

### The Elements of Style
William Strunk and E. B. White
http://amzn.to/TheElementsOfStyle

## Books about Usage

### 101 Misused Words
Mignon Fogarty
http://amzn.to/101MisusedWords

*The Accidents of Style:*
*Good Advice on How Not to Write Badly*
Charles Harrington Elster
http://amzn.to/TheAccidentsOfStyle

*Right, Wrong, and Risk*
*A Dictionary of Today's American English Usage*
Mark Davidson
http://amzn.to/RightWrongRisky

*Simple and Direct*
Jacques Barzun
http://amzn.to/SimpleAndDirect

## Books About Sentences

*Stunning Sentences*
Bruce Ross-Larson
http://amzn.to/StunningSentences

*It Was the Best of Sentences, It Was the Worst of Sentences*
June Casagrande
http://amzn.to/BestOfSentences

*I Never Metaphor I Didn't Like*
Mardy Grothe
http://amzn.to/INeverMetaphorIDidntLike

## Books About Grammar

*Woe is I*
Patricia T. O'Conner
http://amzn.to/WoeIsI

## Books About Punctuation

*The New Well-Tempered Sentence*
Karen Elizabeth Gordon
http://amzn.to/NewWellTemperedSentence

*A Dash of Style*
Noah Lukeman
http://amzn.to/ADashOfStyle

# Books About Dialogue

### The Book of Dialogue
Lewis Turco
http://amzn.to/TheBookOfDialogue

# Books About The Craft of Writing

### The First Five Pages:
### A Writer's Guide To Staying Out of the Rejection Pile
Noah Lukeman
http://amzn.to/FirstFivePages

### The Plot Thickens: 8 Ways to Bring Fiction to Life
Noah Lukeman
http://amzn.to/ThePlotThickens

### Writing the Breakout Novel
Donald Maas
http://amzn.to/WritingTheBreakoutNovel

### Beginnings, Middles, and Ends
Nancy Kress
http://amzn.to/BeginningsMiddlesEnds

### Showing and Telling
Laurie Alberts
http://amzn.to/ShowingAndTelling

### Techniques of the Selling Writer
Dwight Swain
http://amzn.to/TechniquesOfTheSellingWriter

### The Fire in Fiction
Donald Maas
http://amzn.to/TheFireInFiction

### The Breakout Novelist:
### Craft and Strategies for Career Fiction Writers
Donald Maas
http://amzn.to/TheBreakoutNovelist

*The Story Template*
Amy Deardon
http://amzn.to/TheStoryTemplate

## Books About eBook Formatting

*Kindle Formatting: The Complete Guide To Formatting Books For The Amazon Kindle*
Joshua Tallent
http://amzn.to/KindleFormatting

*EPUB Straight to the Point:*
*Creating eBooks for the Apple iPad and other eBook-readers*
Elizabeth Castro
http://amzn.to/EPUBstraight

## Miscellaneous Books

*Random House Webster's Unabridged Dictionary*
Random House
http://amzn.to/RandomHouseDictionary

*Flip Dictionary*
Barbara Ann Kipfer
http://amzn.to/FlipDictionary

*The Fine Print of Self-Publishing - Everything You Need to Know About the Costs, Contracts, and Process of Self-Publishing*
Mark Levine
http://amzn.to/TheFinePrint

*The Beethoven Sketches*
Douglas Johnson, Alan Tyson, Robert Winter
http://amzn.to/BeethovenSketches

# Appendix 3
# The Price of Editing

The Editorial Freelancers Association or EFA (http://www.the-efa.org/res/rates.php) is a good place to start to determine how much editing will cost unless you use the techniques in this book to do it yourself. On their website, the prices are listed per hour with the page "pace" provided; common practice defines a page is considered as 250 words.

I convert the EFA's rates to per word in the following list to make it easier for you to calculate the costs. Simply determine your total word count and then multiply that by their per-word fees.

- Basic Copy editing: 1.2 to 3.2 cents per word
  (average = 2.2 cents per word)
- Heavy Copy editing: 3.4 to 10 cents per word
  (average = 6.7 cents per word)
- Substantive or line editing: 3.3 to 24 cents per word
  (average = 13.65 cents per word)
- Developmental editing: 4.8 to 32 cents per word
  (average = 18.4 cents per word)

Using the average rates above, you can calculate the average editing cost for your manuscript:

| Type of edit | 50,000 words | 100,000 words |
|---|---|---|
| Basic Copy editing | $1,100 | $2,200 |
| Heavy Copy editing | $3,350 | $6,700 |
| Substantive or Line editing | $6,825 | $13,650 |
| Developmental editing | $9,200 | $18,400 |

As you can see, editing is expensive. Of course, you might have a friend who is good with grammar "edit" your book for less or for free. I've seen plenty of books edited that way and my response is, "You get what you pay for."

If you look around the web, you will find many people offering to edit books at $6.00 per 250-word page. That works out to 2.4 cents per word, or $1,200 per 50,000 words and $2,400 per 100,000 words. But what sort of editing is it? Is it copy editing, line editing, or developmental editing?

The lowest rate I have seen on the web for anything beyond basic copy editing is 3 cents per word. This comes to $3,000 for 100,000 words, and the number of items repaired by such edits may turn out to be a fraction of those you can fix using the techniques in the book you hold in your hand: *Final Edit—The Final Hours of your Final Draft.*

When it comes to the editing services of large POD mills, remember, they publish anything submitted, sight unseen; and this means "manuscript unseen by human eyes"—unless you pay an extra fee for that privilege. Such online duplication outlets posing as digital publishers can charge as low as a penny a word for basic copy editing, although most hover around 2.2 to 3.2 cents per word. That is similar to or more than the AFE average rate. However, the sample edits they provide reveal that their definition of the word "basic" is strict. Line editing and developmental editing services offered as add-ons to POD packages tend to be lower than the average AFE rates. I have seen 2.9 cents per word for line editing, 3.5 to 4.2 cents per word for "content editing" (presumably, some sort of substantial editing, but not developmental editing), and 6.4 to 8.4 cents per word for developmental editing.

# Highlighted Quotations

1) Thoreau, Henry David
   Great-Quotes.com, Gledhill Enterprises, 2011.
   Retrieved from:
      http://www.great-quotes.com/quote/140783

2) Zinsser, William Knowlton. *On Writing Well: The Classic Guide to Writing Nonfiction*. New York: HarperCollins, 2006

3) Kilian, Crawford
   *Advice on Novel Writing*
   Retrieved from
      http://www.darkwaves.com/sfch/writing/ckilian/

4) Sand, George
   BrainyQuote.com, Xplore Inc, 2011.
   Retrieved from:
      http://www.brainyquote.com

5) Seuss, Theodore Seuss Geisel (Dr. Seuss)
   Great-Quotes.com, Gledhill Enterprises, 2011.
   Retrieved from:
      http://www.great-quotes.com/quote/2214230

# Index to Searches

## Chapter 3: **Introducing Search**

Global 3-Step Return Replacement
Single-Option Replacement
Double-Option Replacement

## Chapter 4: **Paragraphs and Sentences**

1a) Global Double-space Replacement (Without the Special Menu)
1b) Global Double-space Replacement (Using the Special Menu)
2) Global or Selective Manual Line Break Replacement
3) Global 3-step Return Replacement
4a) Global Space Before Paragraph Mark Replacement
4b) Global Paragraph Mark Followed by Space Replacement
5) Selective Paragraph Termination Search
6) Global Tab Removal
7) Selective Paragraph Capitalization Repair
8) Selective Quoted Paragraph Second Character Repair
9) Selective Sentence Capitalization Repair

## Chapter 5: **Problematic Punctuation**

10a) Global Sentence Terminator Repair
10b) Global Phrase and Clause Punctuation Repair
10c) Global Sentence, Phrase, and Clause Punctuation (Combined)
11a) Global Straight to Curly Quotes Replacement (Normal)
11b) Global or Selective Restoration of Inches and/or Feet
12a) Global Multi-Stage Em Dash Replacement (Preliminary)
12b) Global Multi-Stage Em Dash Replacement (Main Operation)
12c) Global Multi-Stage Em Dash Replacement (Precautionary)
13a) Global Multi-Stage Ellipsis Replacement

13b) Global Multi-Stage Ellipsis Replacement (Precautionary)
13c) Selective Multi-Stage Ellipsis Replacement (Special Cases)
14a) Global En Dash Replacement (Numeric Ranges)
14b) Optional Global En Dash Replacement (Negative Numbers)
14c) Optional Global En Dash Replacement (Days of The Week)
14d) Optional Selective En Dash Replacement (Ranges of Months)
14e) Optional Selective En Dash Replacement (Most Others)
14f) Optional Selective En Dash Replacement (The Rest)
15a) Global Quote Plus Period or Comma Transposition
15b) Optional Selective Parenthesized Citation Repair
15c) Global Quote Plus Semicolon or Colon Transposition
15d.1) Selective 3-Step Quote After Punctuation Transpose (Step 1)
15d.2) Selective 3-Step Quote After Punctuation Transpose (Step 2)
15d.3) Global 3-Step Quote After Punctuation Transposition (Step 3)

## Chapter 6: **Dealing with Dialogue**

16) Selective Capitalized "Said" Inspection and Repair
17) Selective "Said" with Missing Quotation Mark (Precautionary)
18a) Global or Selective "Said" with One-Word Character Name
18b) Selective "Said" with Two-Word Character Name
19) Global "Said She" and "Said He" Transposition
20) Selective "Said" with Articles and Possessives Repair

### *Asked*

21a) Global or Selective "Asked" with One-Word Character Name
21b) Selective "Asked" with Two-Word Character Name

### *Dialogue Proportions*

22a) Dialogue Proportion Analysis (Step 1): Total Dialogue Blocks
22b) Dialogue Proportion Analysis (Step 2): Total with "Said"
22c) Dialogue Proportion Analysis (Step 3): Total with "Asked"

### *Alternate Dialogue Verbs*

23a) Multi-Step Non-"Said" Dialogue Verb Replacements (Step 1)
23b) Multi-Step Non-"Said" Dialogue Verb Replacements (Step 2)
23c) Multi-Step Non-"Said" Dialogue Verb Replacements (Step 3)

## *Additional Dialogue Details*

24) Selective Multi-Paragraph Dialogue Check
25) Selective Attributions Opening Paragraphs Revision
26) Selective Proper Use of Em Dashes & Ellipses in Dialogue Check
27) Selective Dialogue Attribution Adverbs Check
28) Selective Dialogue with Present Participles Check
29) Selective Interior Monologue Check

## Chapter 7: **Down for the Count**

Searching to Count Occurrences

## Chapter 8: **Search and Rapid Rewrite**

30a) Targeting Paragraph Starters is/was/were/seemed (There and It)
30b) Targeting Paragraph Starters is/was/were/seemed (He and She)
30c) Targeting Paragraph Starters is/was/were/seemed (Characters)
31a) Targeting Sentence Starters is/was/were/seemed (There and It)
31b) Targeting Sentence Starters is/was/were/seemed (He and She)
31c) Targeting Sentence Starters with it/was/were/seemed (Characters)
32) Targeting Paragraph & Sentence Starters: Variations of #30 & #31
33a) Targeting More Objectionable Paragraph Starters (pronouns)
33b) Targeting More Objectionable Paragraph Starters (possessives)
33c) Targeting More Objectionable Paragraph Starters (conjunctions)
33d) Targeting More Objectionable Paragraph Starters (misc.)
34) Targeting Chapter Openings with Variations of Search #33
35) Targeting Openings Following a Hiatus: Variations of Search #33

## *Power Position*

36) Targeting Chapter Endings for Power Position Effect
37) Targeting Section (Chunk) Endings

## *Showing vs. Telling*

38) Targeting Verbs of Awareness
39a) Targeting Verbs of Initiation
39b) Targeting Specific Distancing Constructions

## Chapter 9: **Substitution Searches**

40a) Optional "Worst of the Worst" Words and Phrases
40b) Optional "Worst of the Worst" Verbs of Awareness & Initiation
41) Trim Flab Phrases
42a) Vanquish Vague Words
42b) Conquer Ambiguous Contractions
43) Remove Redundancies
44) Banish the Boring
45) Plunder Plague Words

## Chapter 10: **Advanced Searches**

46) Target Nominalizations
47) Target Adverbs Ending in "ly"
48a) Reflexive Pronouns vs. Nominative and Objective Pronouns
48b) Nominative Case Pronouns vs. Objective Case Pronouns
49a) Target Possible Passive Voice
49b) Target Extraneous past perfect
49c) Target Second Word in Sentence = "had" or "was"
49d) Target Second Word in Sentence = "seemed" or "appeared"
50) Target Nonrestrictive Appositives, Phrases, and Clauses

### *Use Your Imagination*

Example 1: Problems with Italics
Example 2: Non-capitalized Days of the Week
Example 3: All Caps Indicates Shouting
Example 4: Former Article Remains After Change of Noun
Example 5: An or an Followed by a Vowel
Example 6: Commonly Confused Words
Example 7: Comma-delineated List Problems

## Chapter 11: **Final Steps**

Use Find & Replace to Automate Style Assignment

# About the Author

**Chris Yavelow** is an award-winning author who has worked in every aspect of the book business, from typesetting to layout and design; from being an editor, publisher, and agent; to developing software for writers.

Yavelow's professional involvement with books began as a teenager setting metal type for printing presses. He was required to memorize the upper case and lower case in order to set type blindfolded. These were wooden cases filled with metal type.

He has worked as a professional writer since the 1980s, starting with small pieces for specialized journals, and eventually writing features and cover stories for national magazines. He now has more than a dozen books to his credit.

After his *Music and Sound Bible* received the Computer Press Association's "Best Advanced How-To Book" award, he spent five years as series editor for A-R Editions' Digital Audio Series.

Since 2000, he has been developing an unprecedented software tool for authors: FictionFixer.com. In 2007, he launched YAV Publications, an author-friendly P.O.D. publishing company with exceptionally high standards. At the time of this writing, he teaches online for the University of Maryland University College.

Chris Yavelow lives in Asheville, North Carolina with his wife Laura. He has two adult daughters.

Email Chris Yavelow at Chris@ScienceOfWriting.com

Postal address:     Chris Yavelow
                    P.O. Box 243
                    Skyland, NC 28776

# FictionFixer

Many of the assertions made in *Final Edit* are based upon research acquired from the author's program FictionFixer.

FictionFixer tracks and analyzes more than 250 characteristics of current bestselling novels. The software combines this data with a consensus of expert advice and opinion to define a model representing what the public expects from such books.

FictionFixer can match every corresponding aspect of an author's manuscript to the current model, a specific work, or both.

Processing a draft through FictionFixer can alert the author to even the most slippery of errors, compared to which, the errors discussed in this book are the tip of the iceberg.

Because FictionFixer is unique among available writing software, it is difficult to explain briefly. Visit FictionFixer.com for more information.

# Would you like a chance to win a free copy of the next edition of this book?

We are giving away 10 copies of the next edition of this book and we are looking for writing samples that show how the *Final Edit* technique is being used.

If you would like a chance to receive a free copy of the next edition of this book, you can enter our competition by taking the following steps.

We are looking for *Before* and *After* samples, so all you need to do is send a copy of your file before having used the *Final Edit* searches to edit your document, and another copy of your document after having done so.

Optionally, you can enable "Track Changes" by selecting "Highlight Changes" from the "Track Changes" submenu in Word. In the ensuing dialog box, enable "Track changes while editing." But this is not required.

First, create copy of your unedited document so that you can use that to compare with your edited version.

After you have completed editing your document using the steps detailed in *Final Edit—The Final Hours of Your Final Draft*, save your edited document with a different filename. You should now have an original document and your edited document.

With the edited document open, select "Compare Documents" from the "Track Changes" submenu. Choose your unedited backup document as the document to compare to your edited version.

After Word has compared the two documents, Word will create a "Comparison Document." Save this Comparison Document as a separate Word document with the word "Comparison" and your own name somewhere in the filename.

Attach the "Comparison" document to an email to Contest@ScienceOfWriting.com.

**Include in the body of the email, whether you will permit brief examples from your comparison document to be cited in the forthcoming book. Indicate any limitation you have upon such usage."**

**If you do give permission for us to use such instructional examples, also indicate whether you want those examples to remain anonymous.**

Optionally, you can give permission for your name to appear in the footnotes that reference your example in the end matter of the book.

Note, unless you provide the two bits of information requested in **bold**, above, we will assume that you do not give permission for examples from your document to appear in the forthcoming edition. In either case, you will still be entered in the drawing for a free copy of the new edition.

CPSIA information can be obtained at www.ICGtesting.com
Printed in the USA
LVOW092333061111

253741LV00002B/1/P